CABIN COOKIN'

The Very Best Recipes for Beef,
Pork, Poultry, Seafood,
and Wild Game for Dutch Ovens,
Skillets, and Grills

Rick Black

STACKPOLE
BOOKS

Copyright © 2007 by Stackpole Books

Published by
STACKPOLE BOOKS
5067 Ritter Road
Mechanicsburg, PA 17055
www.stackpolebooks.com

Printed in the United States

First edition

10   9   8   7   6   5   4   3   2   1

Cover design by Wendy A. Reynolds
Cover illustration by Daniel Roberts

Library of Congress Cataloging-in-Publication Data
Black, Rick.
  Cabin cookin' : the very best recipes for beef, pork, poultry, seafood, and wild game for dutch ovens, skillets, and grills / Rick Black.
    p. cm.
  Includes index.
  ISBN-13: 978-0-8117-3385-4 (alk. paper)
  ISBN-10: 0-8117-3385-8 (alk. paper)
  1. Cookery. 2. Outdoor cookery. I. Title.

TX652.B58175 2007
641.5—dc22

2006026584

*I dedicate this book to the following hunting, fishing,
and camping buddies:*

Billy Wilke (deer cabin)
Jeff May (deer cabin)
Vinny Moser (turkey/fishing cabin)
Bob Moser (turkey/fishing cabin)
Bob Raid (upland bird cabin)
Kaylen Vickers (deer/turkey/duck/fishing/rabbit cabin)
Buddy Miler (big game cabin)
My son, Travis Black (all of the above)

*It is with the fond memories of the hours we have spent that the
pages of this book will unfold.*

CONTENTS

ACKNOWLEDGMENTS

My thanks for help in furnishing data, photos, and for sharing their time, knowledge, and experience go to Mike Hoffman of Keystone; Brad Holland of the Holland Grill Company (Cousin Rick's grill of choice); Dan Roberts, my cartoonist; Cosmo of the New Mix 107.3 Radio Show; Judith Schnell of Stackpole Books; Terry Lee for my computer support; The Food Guru Chef Peter Harman; Fareway Stores, Inc.; the staff and crew of Martini's Grille for letting me play with their cool stuff; Fleck Sales (the beer boys); Farm King Supply Stores; Robin Delaney of *The Fort Madison Democrat;* Randy Fox of National Studio; *The Keokuk Daily Gate City;* Cris Roberts of *The Burlington Hawkeye;* and the remaining media folks for making this hillbilly look good. And as always special note of thanks also to Amy Lerner for editing the manuscript through all its convolutions with patience and insight and gentle firmness.

Finally, I am ever so grateful for the ongoing love and support of my family—Becky, Shaena, and Travis—from whom I've stolen time to work on this project.

R. B.

INTRODUCTION

Cabin cooks really shouldn't feel bound to rigidly follow another cook's list of ingredients and seasonings. Whether cabin meals are cooked over charcoal or a fire pit in a patio, on a grill or spit or in a Dutch oven or cast-iron skillet in a wilderness cabin, the cook's improvisational touch is what gives them that extra dimension of goodness. Of course, it helps that those who share the cabin are usually as hungry as bears after a day spent outdoors hunting, fishing, or hiking. There are several types of cabin style cooking: Dutch oven, cast-iron skillet, vittles cooked in heavy foil, and, one of my favorites, grilling.

The time of day, the weather, and what I want to cook determine which method I choose to cook with. That is why I wanted to write a cookbook that includes all the methods I have used in the past while camping out in my cabins. In this book you will learn some of my favorite and most popular dishes using Dutch ovens, cast-iron skillets, and foil, and making soups and stews, grilled wild game, and cabin snacks. I even put together some of my tips and tricks for making your life easier while roughing it in the great outdoors.

It would be safe to say that the log cabin is a large part of American history. During the seventeenth and eighteenth centuries, waves of Eastern and Central Europeans, including the Swiss and Germans, came to America, bringing their knowledge of log-home construction. Even the Scotch-Irish, who did not possess a log-building tradition of their own, adapted the form of the stone houses of their native country to log construction and contributed to its spread across the frontier. In the Mississippi Valley, colonial French fur traders and settlers had introduced vertical log construction in the seventeenth century. Through the late eighteenth and early nineteenth centuries, frontier settlers erected log cabins as they cleared land, winding their way south in and along the Appalachian valleys through the backcountry areas of Maryland, Virginia, the Carolinas, and Georgia. They moved westward across the Appalachian Mountain barrier into the Ohio and Mississippi river valleys, transporting their indispensable log craft with them into Kentucky and Tennessee and as far to the southwest as eastern Texas. Log buildings are known to have been constructed as temporary shelters by soldiers during the Revolutionary War, and across the country, Americans used logs to build not only houses, but also commercial structures, schools, churches, gristmills, barns, corncribs, and a variety of outbuildings. So cabin cooking is very much a part of us all.

I love spending every free minute I have hunting and fishing, but no matter what kind of luck I may have afield, nothing puts a smile on my face quicker than smelling good vittles cooking as I approach the cabin campsite.

This book is intended for the outdoorsman in you and is a great tool to help you whip up meals at your cabin campsite. I hope you have as much fun using this book and its recipes as I did writing it.

1

DUTCH-OVEN COOKIN'

Dutch-oven cooking and cabins go together like a musket ball and black powder. Any outdoorsman knows with one you must have the other. In this chapter we will cover some of my favorite Dutch-oven recipes. But first a few tips on the subject.

A Dutch oven is preferably made of cast iron and has a smooth bottom with three short legs for raising it above the heat source. The lid is not as rounded as that of a kitchen pan and has a lip for keeping charcoal on top. I recommend a 16-inch, 12-quart Dutch oven for these recipes. Dutch ovens are invaluable for cabin soups, stews, roasting, and, of course, baking.

There are many ways to clean a Dutch oven. Not all cooks believe you should use soap on your Dutch oven. Some old boys suggest never washing them, others wash them, but not with detergent. I have found that using a few drops of dishwashing soap if you have been cooking something really greasy will not damage a well-seasoned oven. Just be sure to rinse several times to make sure there is no soap residue. If your oven is not well seasoned, whatever you put in the oven will be absorbed into the pot and become part of your next meal.

Dutch-oven care begins with seasoning, but it's important to clean it properly after each use. Cleaning cast iron is easier than scrubbing pots and pans. As soon as possible after cooking with your Dutch oven, scrape out as much food as possible with a plastic scraper. Put 1 to 2 quarts of very hot water in your oven and scrub with a vegetable brush. Immediately after washing it, dry the oven thoroughly.

Opening Day Breakfast Vittles

15 slices bread, cubed
6 tablespoons butter, melted
1 pound shredded cheddar cheese
18 eggs
$^3/_4$ cup milk
1 teaspoon dry mustard
1 teaspoon salt
$^1/_2$ teaspoon black pepper
$^1/_2$ teaspoon garlic powder
1 pound cooked loose sausage

Place the bread cubes in a well-greased Dutch oven. Drizzle butter over the bread, and sprinkle the cheese over the top. Whisk together eggs, milk, and mustard. Season with the salt, pepper, and garlic powder. Pour the egg mixture over the bread and cheese. Sprinkle the cooked sausage over the top. Cover and bake, using 10 briquettes on the bottom and 16 briquettes on the top, for 45 minutes, or until the eggs are set.

Cousin Rick's Cabin Onion Brisket

8 pounds beef brisket, well trimmed

2 teaspoons rosemary

2 bay leaves

2 teaspoons garlic salt

I teaspoon black pepper

4 sliced sweet onions

$^1/_2$ pound sliced mushrooms

3 ribs sliced celery

I chopped red bell pepper

4 minced garlic cloves

2 cups chili sauce

12 ounces dark beer

$^1/_2$ cup beef stock

2 tablespoons brown sugar

2 tablespoons Worcestershire sauce

Place the trimmed brisket, fat side up, in a Dutch oven. Season with the rosemary, bay leaves, garlic salt, and pepper. Arrange the sliced sweet onions, mushrooms, celery, bell pepper, and garlic over the meat. In a mixing bowl, combine the remaining ingredients, whisk well, and then pour the mixture over the top of the meat in the oven. Cover and bake, using 12 briquettes on the bottom and 15 briquettes on the top, for 4 hours, replacing the briquettes every hour. Baste the meat often with the pan drippings. When the meat is done and tender, remove it from the oven and let it rest for 15 minutes, and then carve and serve with the pan juices and onions.

Wapello Cabin Meatloaf

2 cups breadcrumbs
1 cup milk
4 pounds lean ground beef
1 diced yellow onion
3 eggs
1 grated carrot
$1/2$ cup ketchup
$1/2$ cup grated cheddar cheese
2 teaspoons thyme
2 teaspoons marjoram
1 teaspoon oregano
1 teaspoon rosemary
$1/2$ teaspoon ginger
$1/4$ teaspoon cumin
2 teaspoons salt
1 teaspoon Accent
1 teaspoon pepper
8 carrots
6 red potatoes
15 asparagus spears

Pack down the breadcrumbs in a small bowl. Add the milk to the breadcrumbs and allow to absorb. To a large mixing bowl, add the beef, onions, breadcrumbs and milk, eggs, grated carrot, ketchup, cheese, and seasonings. Mix thoroughly using your hands. Place the mixture in a Dutch oven, and form it into a ring against the sides of the oven, leaving a cavity in the center for the vegetables. Cover the top of the meatloaf ring evenly with ketchup. Cut the carrots into halves lengthwise and the potatoes into quarters lengthwise. Trim the bottoms of the asparagus. Line the insides of the meatloaf ring with carrot halves. Inside the carrots stand the potato quarters in a ring. Stand the asparagus spears in the center. Roast using 15 briquettes on top and bottom for 90 minutes. Rotate the Dutch oven and lid every 20 minutes.

Clearlake Cabin Goulash Vittles

1 pound lean ground beef
2 tablespoons olive oil
1 diced yellow onion
1 diced green bell pepper
1 cup fresh sliced mushrooms
2 minced garlic cloves
1 cup frozen corn
$^1/_2$ cup sliced olives
2 10-ounce cans tomato soup
$2^1/_2$ soup cans hot water
$^1/_2$ teaspoon cayenne
$^1/_4$ teaspoon paprika
2 teaspoons salt
1 teaspoon pepper
12-ounce package pasta shells
3 cups grated cheddar cheese

Brown the ground beef in the olive oil in a Dutch oven using 25 briquettes bottom heat. When the beef has browned, add the onion, bell pepper, mushrooms, and garlic. Sauté until the peppers are tender. Add the corn, olives, tomato soup, hot water, paprika, cayenne, salt, and pepper. Stir to mix well. Bring the mixture to a boil and then stir in the pasta shells. Place the lid on the Dutch oven, and bake, using 15 briquettes bottom and 15 briquettes top heat, for about 40 minutes. Sprinkle the cheese over top, and bake for another 15 minutes. Serve when the cheese is good and melted.

Bear Lodge Taters and Meat

2 pounds lean ground beef

1 diced yellow onion

6 minced garlic cloves

1 teaspoon salt

1 teaspoon pepper

2 pounds frozen tater tots

2 10-ounce cans cream of mushroom soup

1 10-ounce can cream of chicken soup

3 tablespoons Worcestershire sauce

1 tablespoon soy sauce

2 teaspoons marjoram

2 teaspoons thyme

4 cups shredded Colby Jack cheese

Heat a Dutch oven using 25 briquettes on the bottom until the oven is hot. Add the ground beef, onions, and garlic to the oven, season with salt and pepper, and fry until the beef is brown and the onions are tender. Remove the ground beef and onion mixture from the oven, and place in a large bowl. Layer 1 pound of tater tots in the bottom of oven. In another bowl, mix together the soups, Worcestershire sauce, soy sauce, thyme, and marjoram. Spoon this mixture into the ground beef mixture and mix well. Spoon half of the ground beef mixture over the tater tots. Sprinkle half of the cheese over the ground beef. Layer again with the remaining pound of tater tots, the rest of the ground beef mixture, and remaining cheese. Cover and cook for about 90 minutes, using 15 briquettes on the bottom and 15 briquettes on the top, rotating the oven and lid every 10 minutes. Serve hot.

Lip Smackin' Ribs

8 pounds beef back ribs, well trimmed of fat
Sidewinder rub (from my *Grillin' Like a Villain* cookbook), to taste
12 ounces My Old Dogs Be Hurtin' BBQ sauce
   (from my *Grillin' Like a Villain* cookbook)
12 ounces chili sauce
4 minced garlic cloves
4 tablespoons dry minced onion
1 tablespoon Accent
2 teaspoons red pepper flakes

Separate the ribs into single rib pieces by cutting between the bones. Trim excess fat from both skin and membrane sides of each rib. Season the ribs with Sidewinder rub, and then place them in a large Ziploc bag and chill for 1 hour. Arrange the ribs in a Dutch oven. In a large bowl, mix together the remaining ingredients, and spoon over the ribs. Cover oven and bake, using 12 briquettes on the bottom and 18 briquettes on the top, for about 2 hours. Baste with the pan drippings every 20 minutes. Replenish the briquettes every hour to keep oven good and hot.

Jeff May's Beef Brisket

6 pounds beef brisket, well trimmed of fat
6 minced garlic cloves
2 tablespoons onion salt
2 tablespoons celery salt
1 tablespoon black pepper
4 tablespoons liquid smoke
3 pounds sliced yellow onions
$^1/_2$ cup chili sauce
$^1/_2$ cup brown sugar
$^1/_2$ cup Worcestershire sauce
1 cup beer

Place the brisket in a large glass dish. Sprinkle the garlic, salts, pepper, and 3 tablespoons of liquid smoke over both sides of the beef, and then hand rub over all. Return to fat side up, and then arrange the onion slices over the top. Cover the dish, and let chill for 24 hours. In a Dutch oven, combine the chili sauce, brown sugar, Worcestershire sauce, beer, and remaining liquid smoke. Heat using 12 briquettes on the bottom, and let simmer until all the sugar has dissolved. Place the sauce in a glass bowl. Place the brisket in the oven, and arrange the onions back over the top. Pour half the sauce over the brisket; then cover and bake, using 15 briquettes on the bottom and 10 briquettes on the top, for about 5 hours. When the beef is tender, remove it from the oven and allow it to rest for 10 minutes. Slice the brisket thinly across the grain, and dip the slices in the remaining sauce.

Terry Lee's Dutch-Oven Sausages

4 pounds browned Italian sausages
26 ounces spaghetti sauce
2 sliced yellow onions
2 sliced green bell peppers
5 minced garlic cloves
2 teaspoons dried basil
2 teaspoons dried oregano

Combine all the ingredients together in a Dutch oven, and stir to mix well. Place the lid on the oven and bake, using 10 briquettes on the bottom and 16 briquettes on the top, for about 2 hours.

Farm King Potatoes

$^1/_2$ cup butter
1 pound lean ground beef
1 diced yellow onion
6 grated red potatoes
1 10-ounce can cream of chicken soup
1 cup sour cream
1 cup grated cheddar cheese
$^1/_2$ cup milk
1 teaspoon Accent
1 teaspoon white pepper
$^1/_2$ cup cracker crumbs

Preheat the Dutch oven using 25 briquettes on the bottom. When the oven is good and hot, add the butter, ground beef, and onions. Sauté until the beef is brown and the onions are tender. Add the potatoes, and stir to mix well. Place the lid on the Dutch oven, and bake, using 15 briquettes on the bottom and 18 briquettes on the top, for about 20 minutes, or until the potatoes start to soften. In a bowl, combine the soup, sour cream, cheddar cheese, and milk. Stir to mix. Season with Accent and white pepper. Pour soup mixture over the potatoes, and stir to mix. Sprinkle the cracker crumbs over the potatoes. Replace the lid, and bake for another 40 minutes.

Jim Hartschuh's Polish Sausage

4 pounds smoked Polish sausages, cut into 1-inch slices
2 sliced white onions
2 cups brown sugar
1/2 cup spicy mustard
5 minced garlic cloves
1 cup beer

Place the sausages and onions in a Dutch oven. In a bowl, combine the remaining ingredients together, and mix well. Pour the mixture over the sausages and onions, and stir to mix. Place the lid on the oven, and bake, using 10 briquettes on the bottom and 16 briquettes on the top, for about an hour, stirring every 20 minutes. Serve hot and seasoned to taste.

Wayne's Cabin on the River Roast of Pork

1 crown roast of pork
3 tablespoons olive oil
12 ounces frozen apple juice concentrate
2 cinnamon sticks
6 whole cloves
2 teaspoons rosemary
1 teaspoon thyme
10 whole peppercorns

Seasoning Mix

1 tablespoon paprika
1 teaspoon onion salt
1 teaspoon garlic powder with parsley
1 teaspoon thyme
1/2 teaspoon rosemary
1/2 teaspoon sage
1/2 teaspoon celery seed
2 teaspoons salt
1 teaspoon pepper

In a bowl, combine the paprika, onion salt, garlic powder, thyme, rosemary, sage, celery seed, salt, and pepper. Mix well. Pat the roast dry of all excess moisture. Rub the roast all over with the olive oil and then apply the seasoning mix. Work the mix well into the roast. Place the seasoned roast in a large plastic bag, and let it chill for 24 hours. Let the roast stand at room temperature for 30 minutes prior to cooking. Wrap the ends of the ribs with foil to prevent them from burning. Place a crumpled piece of foil into the center of the roast. In a Dutch oven, add the apple juice concentrate, cinnamon sticks, cloves, rosemary, thyme, and peppercorns. Bring to a slow boil using 25 briquettes on the bottom. Place the roast in the oven, and cook using 15 briquettes on the bottom and 15 briquettes on the top, basting often with drippings. Cook the roast until the internal meat temperature reaches 170 degrees. Remove the roast from the oven, and let sit for 10 minutes before serving.

Cabin Mist Baked Chops

1 package quick pork stuffing
4 tablespoons melted butter
1 cup hot water
1 20-ounce can sliced peaches
6 pork chops
Salt and pepper
$1/4$ cup apricot preserves
1 tablespoon Dijon mustard
1 tablespoon dry minced onion

In a Dutch oven, add the stuffing mix, butter, water, and juice from the peaches; stir to mix, and then spread evenly. Season the chops with salt and pepper and arrange over the top of the stuffing. In a bowl, mix together the preserves, mustard, and minced onion. Spoon preserves mixture over top of chops, and spread to coat. Arrange the sliced peaches on top of all. Cover and bake, using 15 briquettes on the bottom and 20 briquettes on the top, for about 60 minutes.

Timber Ghost Chicken Meal

2 cups long grain rice
1 10-ounce can cream of mushroom soup
1 10-ounce can cream of chicken soup
1 cup sour cream
1 diced yellow onion
1 diced celery stalk
3 minced garlic cloves
2 tablespoons Worcestershire sauce
2 soup cans water
10 pieces chicken
2 teaspoons poultry seasoning
1 teaspoon black pepper

In a Dutch oven, combine the rice, soups, sour cream, onion, celery, garlic, Worcestershire sauce, and water. Mix well. Season chicken with poultry seasoning and pepper. Place the chicken over rice mixture in oven. Cover the oven and bake, using 15 briquettes on the bottom and 20 briquettes on the top, for 90 minutes.

Cabin Critter Chicken

10 skinless chicken thighs
$2/3$ cup ketchup
$2/3$ cup chutney
2 tablespoons olive oil
3 tablespoons minced red onion
2 minced garlic cloves
1 teaspoon salt
1 teaspoon pepper
2 teaspoons Louisiana hot sauce
$1/4$ cup lemon juice

Place the chicken meat in a Dutch oven. In a bowl, combine the ketchup, chutney, olive oil, garlic, onion, salt, pepper, Louisiana hot sauce, and lemon juice. Pour this sauce over the chicken, and then cover the oven. Bake, using 10 briquettes on the bottom and 20 briquettes on the top, for about 75 minutes. Serve chicken over rice.

Kenny's Cabin Ribs

2 tablespoons vegetable oil
2 pounds boneless pork spare ribs, cut into 2-inch pieces
6 green onions, cut into 1-inch pieces
1 tablespoon dry sherry
2 tablespoons white vinegar
3 tablespoons sugar
4 tablespoons soy sauce
5 tablespoons water

Heat a well-oiled Dutch oven, using 25 briquettes on the bottom, until hot. Add the oil and spare-rib meat; sear ribs on all sides until brown. Add the green onions. Mix together the remaining ingredients, and then pour over the browned meat. Bring liquid to a low boil; then cover the oven with the lid, and simmer for about 45 minutes, using 15 briquettes on the bottom and 12 briquettes on the top, stirring every 15 minutes. Serve rib meat over steamed rice.

Hawkeye Dutch-Oven Potatoes

1 pound thick-sliced bacon
2 sliced yellow onions
5 minced garlic cloves
2 cups sliced mushrooms
12 red potatoes, peeled and sliced
1 10-ounce can cream of chicken soup
1 10-ounce can cheddar cheese soup
1 cup sour cream
2 tablespoons Worcestershire sauce
1 tablespoon soy sauce
1 teaspoon salt
1 teaspoon white pepper

Heat the Dutch oven using 25 briquettes on the bottom until the oven is good and hot. Cut the bacon into 1-inch slices, and fry them in the oven until brown. Add the onions, garlic, and mushrooms. Stir; then cover and cook until the onions are tender. Add the potatoes. In a large bowl, combine the remaining ingredients, and mix well. Pour soup mixture over the potatoes, and stir until all the potatoes are well coated. Cover and cook for about an hour, using 15 briquettes on the bottom and 15 briquettes on the top. Stir the pot gently every 10 minutes.

Bubba's Dutch-Oven Beans

2 pounds pinto beans, soaked for 12 hours

10 cups hot water

24 ounces cola

3/4 cup ketchup

1/4 cup Worcestershire sauce

1/4 cup steak sauce (any one of my sauces from *Grillin' Like a Villain*)

1 30-ounce can whole tomatoes

2 diced yellow onions

8 minced garlic cloves

1 pound thick-sliced bacon, cut into 1-inch pieces

6 tablespoons chili powder

3 minced Serrano peppers

4 teaspoons toasted caraway seeds, ground

Add all the ingredients to the Dutch oven. Bring to a boil using 25 briquettes on the bottom, stirring the beans frequently. Cover the beans, and continue to simmer, using 10 briquettes on the bottom and 15 briquettes on the top, for 3 hours. Stir the beans from the bottom up every 20 minutes. Add additional water if the beans begin to dry out. The beans should be soft but not weak in texture.

Larry Humphrey's Fort Madison Beans

1 pound lean ground beef
1/2 pound bacon
1 diced yellow onion
1 diced green bell pepper
1/2 cup brown sugar
1/2 cup ketchup
16 ounces chili sauce
2 tablespoons prepared mustard
1/2 pound precooked ham, cubed
2 31-ounce cans pork and beans

Heat the Dutch oven using 25 briquettes on the bottom until the oven is good and hot. Add the beef, and cook until brown. Remove the beef, and drain all fat. Cut the bacon into 1-inch slices, and fry in oven until brown. Add the onions and green bell pepper, and sauté until the onions are tender. Drain off excess fat. Reduce the briquettes on the bottom to 12. Add the browned beef, brown sugar, ketchup, chili sauce, and mustard. Simmer for 20 minutes. Add the ham and beans. Cover, and add about 15 briquettes to the lid. Simmer for 2 hours, stirring every 20 minutes.

Branson Chicken Pot Pie

4 boneless, skinless chicken breasts, diced
3 tablespoons olive oil
4 minced garlic cloves
1 diced yellow onion
4 red potatoes, diced
1 16-ounce package frozen mixed vegetables, thawed
2 10-ounce cans cream of chicken soup
$^1/_2$ cup evaporated milk
2 teaspoons poultry seasoning
Salt and pepper
2 tablespoons Worcestershire sauce
1 can refrigerated crescent rolls

Heat the Dutch oven, using 25 briquettes on the bottom, until hot. Add chicken, olive oil, and garlic to the hot oven; season with salt and pepper to taste. Cook the chicken, stirring often, until the chicken is no longer pink. Add the onions and potatoes, and continue cooking until the onions are tender. Stir in the mixed vegetables, soup, milk, poultry seasoning, and Worcestershire sauce; season with salt and pepper. Let the mixture come to a low boil. Unroll the crescent rolls, and create a top crust by layering flat rolls across the top of the ingredients. Reduce the heat on the bottom to 10 briquettes, and add 18 briquettes to the lid. Bake for 35 minutes until the rolls are brown and flaky. Check to make sure the potatoes are cooked through.

Mountain Man Christmas Turkey

Turkey

1 15-pound fresh or thawed turkey
1 bay leaf
1 quartered yellow onion
2 sliced garlic cloves
6 pressed garlic cloves
1 cup warm water

Basting Sauce

$^1/_2$ cup butter, melted
1 teaspoon dried mint leaves
1 teaspoon thyme
$^1/_2$ teaspoon sage
$^1/_2$ teaspoon marjoram
$^1/_2$ teaspoon sweet basil
1 teaspoon celery salt
1 teaspoon salt
1 teaspoon pepper

Mashed Potatoes

8 red potatoes, peeled and sliced
$^1/_4$ cup butter
$^1/_4$ cup milk

Gravy

2 tablespoons cornstarch
$^1/_2$ cup water
Drippings from Dutch oven

Rinse turkey, making sure it is thawed completely. Pat dry. Twist the wings in behind. Place the bay leaf, quartered onion, and sliced garlic into the cavity of the turkey. Rub the pressed garlic all over the outside skin of the turkey. Place the turkey into Dutch oven. Pour 1 cup of warm water into the bottom of the Dutch oven. Cover and cook, using 20 briquettes on the bottom and 30 briquettes on the top. Prepare the basting sauce in a small dish by adding herbs to melted butter. Stir until well blended. Brush the turkey with the basting sauce often as the turkey cooks. Replace the coals every 45 minutes until the meat thermometer inserted into the breast of the turkey reads 175 degrees. Arrange the potatoes in the bottom of the Dutch oven around the turkey about 1 hour before meat is done cooking. When the potatoes are cooked, remove them from the oven, and mash them with the butter and milk. Season with garlic salt and pepper. When the turkey is done, remove it from the Dutch oven. Increase the briquettes on bottom of the Dutch oven to 30. Stir the cornstarch in $1/2$ cup water until dissolved. Whisk cornstarch mixture into the drippings in the Dutch oven. Stir until the mixture comes to a boil. Season the gravy with salt and pepper. Let the turkey rest for 10 minutes before carving.

Shaky Pistols Crandall's Dutch-Oven BBQ Sauce

2 tablespoons olive oil
5 minced garlic cloves
3 cups chili sauce
$1/2$ cup brown sugar
$1/2$ cup Worcestershire sauce
$1/3$ cup red wine vinegar
$1/4$ cup beer
1 teaspoon celery salt
1 teaspoon onion salt
1 teaspoon pepper
1 teaspoon Louisiana hot sauce
2 tablespoons liquid smoke

Heat the Dutch oven using 15 briquettes on the bottom until hot. Add the olive oil and garlic, and sauté for about 1 minute, stirring very often so garlic does not burn. Add the remaining ingredients, and bring to a low boil. Reduce the briquettes on bottom to 8, and let sauce simmer for about 30 minutes. Use this sauce for beef, pork, chicken, and venison.

Stagecoach Stopover Biscuits

4 cups flour
2 tablespoons baking powder
I teaspoon salt
$^1/_2$ cup lard (or shortening)
2 cups cold milk

In a mixing bowl, add the flour, baking powder, and salt. Stir together using a fork. Cut in the lard until the mixture is like a course meal with no lumps. Add the milk, and stir until all the flour is absorbed. Dough should be sticky and moist. Generously flour a large cutting board, making sure to coat your hands also. Scoop the dough from the bowl, and place it on the floured board. Press down on the dough until the dough is equal in thickness and the shape of an oval. Fold the dough and repeat the pressing steps 8 times, adding flour as needed to keep the dough from sticking. Pat the kneaded dough into a circular shape about half an inch thick. Using a 2-inch biscuit cutter, cut out the biscuits by pressing the cutter into the dough and then lifting it straight out. Place the biscuits in a greased Dutch oven leaving a $\frac{1}{2}$-inch gap between each. Place the lid on the oven, and let the biscuits rise for 12 minutes. Bake the biscuits, using 15 briquettes on the bottom and 25 briquettes on the top, for about 20 minutes.

Salt Lick Creek Cornbread

I $^1/_2$ cups sourdough starter
2$^1/_4$ cups canned milk
2$^1/_4$ cups yellow cornmeal
3 tablespoons sugar
3 beaten eggs
6 teaspoons melted butter
I teaspoon baking soda
I teaspoon salt

In a large bowl, combine the sourdough starter, milk, cornmeal, sugar, and eggs; stir well. Add the melted butter, baking soda, and salt; stir until well mixed. Turn the mixture into a lightly greased Dutch oven and spread out evenly. Place lid on Dutch oven, and bake, using 15 briquettes on the bottom and 25 briquettes on the top, for 30 minutes, or until the cornbread turns golden brown. Great with Hunter Ham and Beans!

Whiskey Willie's Cabin #12 Cornbread Recipe

1 cup butter
4 beaten eggs
3 cups milk
2 cups sugar
2 cups cornmeal
3 cups flour
4 teaspoons baking powder
1 teaspoon garlic salt
1 teaspoon Accent
1 teaspoon white pepper

In a large bowl, combine the butter, eggs, and milk. In a separate bowl sift together the sugar, cornmeal, flour, baking powder, garlic salt, Accent, and white pepper. Mix the dry ingredients into the wet ingredients about a cup at a time until well blended. Spoon the cornbread mixture into a lightly greased Dutch oven, and spread evenly. Cover the Dutch oven and bake, using 10 briquettes on the bottom and 20 briquettes on the top, for about 45 minutes, or until golden brown.

IANG 224th Johnny Cakes

4 cups sour milk
4 beaten eggs
$1/4$ cup melted butter
4 cups cornmeal
2 cups flour
2 cups whole wheat flour
$1/3$ cup sugar
2 teaspoons baking soda
I teaspoon baking powder
I teaspoon salt

In a large Army mixing bowl, combine together the milk, eggs, and butter. In a separate Army mixing bowl, sift the cornmeal, flours, sugar, baking soda, baking powder, and salt. Mix the dry ingredients into the wet ingredients, and blend well. Spoon mixture into an oiled Dutch oven, and spread out evenly. Cover the Dutch oven and bake, using 12 briquettes on the bottom and 20 briquettes on the top, for about 50 minutes, or until the cake comes out golden brown.

Burlington Mississippi Cabin-Cooked Mud Cake

I package of yellow cake mix; prepared as directed

Topping

I 10-ounce package semisweet chocolate chips
$3/4$ cup chopped pecans
$1/2$ cup powdered sugar

Mud

$1/2$ cup cocoa powder
2 cups brown sugar
I cup hot water
2 teaspoons vanilla
I teaspoon cinnamon

Line the bottom and sides of the Dutch oven with heavy foil. Add the prepared cake mix to the oven. Prepare the mud mixture in a separate bowl by combining all the ingredients together, and mix well. Add the mud ingredients over the cake mixture in the oven. Cover the Dutch oven, and bake, using 12 briquettes on the bottom and 18 briquettes on the top, for about 60 minutes. Sprinkle the chocolate chips and pecans over the cake about 5 minutes before the cake is done baking. Dust the top of the cake with the powdered sugar just before serving.

Mountain Monster Cookies

I cup melted butter
I cup brown sugar
$^1/_2$ cup sugar
2 eggs
I teaspoon vanilla
I $^1/_2$ cups flour
I $^1/_4$ teaspoons baking soda
I teaspoon salt
3 cups oats
I cup minced coconut
I cup raisins
$^1/_2$ cup chocolate chips
$^1/_2$ cup chopped pecans
$^1/_2$ cup chopped walnuts

In a large bowl, mix together the butter, sugars, eggs, and vanilla. Stir in the flour, baking soda, salt, and oats, mixing well. Stir in the remaining ingredients. Lightly oil the Dutch oven. Using a tablespoon, drop the cookie dough in small balls about 2 inches apart into the Dutch oven. Cover and bake, using 15 briquettes on the bottom and 18 briquettes on the top, for about 15 minutes or until the tops of the cookies just start turning brown. Remove the cookies from the oven by using a pancake turner, and let them cool. Repeat the baking process until all cookies are made.

Sweet Pea Phylis Hoffman's Pancakes

1 1/2 cups milk
9 eggs
1 1/2 cups flour
2 tablespoons blueberries
3/4 teaspoon salt
6 tablespoons butter
2 tablespoons lemon juice
2 tablespoons powdered sugar

In a large mixing bowl, whisk together the milk, eggs, flour, blueberries, and salt to form a thin batter. Heat the Dutch oven, using 18 briquettes on the bottom and 20 briquettes on the top, until the oven is very hot. Add butter to the oven, and let it melt. Pour all the batter into the oven, and cook for about 30 minutes, or until the pancake is lightly browned and done. Sprinkle the pancake with lemon juice, and dust with the powdered sugar.

Sunday Morning Spice Cake

8 Granny Smith apples, peeled, cored, sliced, and quartered
1/2 cup raisins
1/2 cup chopped walnuts
1 cup brown sugar
2 tablespoons flour
1 teaspoon cinnamon
1 teaspoon nutmeg
1 package spice cake mix, prepared as directed

In the Dutch oven, add the apples, raisins, walnuts, brown sugar, flour, cinnamon, and nutmeg. Stir until all the ingredients are well mixed and the apples are coated. Pour the prepared spice cake batter over top of apples and spread evenly. Bake, using 12 briquettes on the bottom and 18 briquettes on the top, for about 60 minutes, or until the top center of the cake springs back when touched.

Elk Chili

1^1/$_2$ pounds ground elk
2 cans dark red kidney beans
1 large onion, chopped
2 large stalks celery, chopped
1 tablespoon chili powder
1 teaspoon salt
1 15-ounce can tomato sauce
1 teaspoon cumin
^{1}/$_2$ teaspoon Accent
1 teaspoon minced garlic
Miller Lite beer

Brown the meat in a Dutch oven. Add the remaining ingredients, adding a little Miller Lite beer if the chili is too thick. Simmer for about 1½ hours, making sure it does not get too dry. Serve with crackers or grated cheese and onions.

Elk Royale Soup

2 pounds ground elk
$1/2$ teaspoon salt
$1/4$ teaspoon pepper
$1/8$ teaspoon garlic powder
6 chicken bouillon cubes
6 beef bouillon cubes
7 cups water
2 cups Miller Lite beer
10-ounce package frozen peas
10-ounce package frozen corn
1 medium diced onion
3 stalks diced celery
5 sliced carrots
4 diced potatoes
2 sliced parsnips
1 sliced turnip
1 teaspoon basil
$1/4$ teaspoon oregano
$1/4$ teaspoon parsley
1 bay leaf

Brown the meat in a Dutch oven with salt, pepper, and garlic powder. Dissolve the bouillon cubes in water and beer, and add to oven. Add the remaining ingredients. Cover the oven, and simmer until the veggies are tender, stirring occasionally, about 1 hour. Discard the bay leaf before serving.

Southwestern Chili

2 large onions, chopped

2 green bell peppers, cored, seeded, and chopped

2 tablespoons (3 large cloves) garlic

3 tablespoons vegetable oil

1/4 cup chili powder, or to taste

1 tablespoon ground cumin

1 tablespoon dried oregano

2 tablespoons tomato paste

3 pounds ground elk

1 28-ounce can whole tomatoes with liquid

1 1/2 cups beef broth

4 tablespoons cider vinegar

1 ounce unsweetened chocolate, chopped

1 19-ounce can kidney beans, rinsed and drained

Rice, as an accompaniment

Toppings: Tortilla chips, sour cream, grated cheddar, chopped red onions, chopped jalapeños, diced avocado, minced cilantro, etc.

In a 9⅓-quart Dutch oven, sauté the onions, peppers, and garlic in oil over moderate heat, stirring occasionally, for about 5 minutes. Add the chili powder, cumin, and oregano, and cook, stirring, for about 3 minutes. Add the tomato paste, and cook, stirring, for about 2 minutes. Add the meat, and cook, stirring occasionally, until meat is no longer pink. Add the tomatoes, 1 cup of the broth, vinegar, and chocolate, and bring the mixture to a boil, crushing the tomatoes with the back of a large wooden spoon. Simmer, covered, for about 1 hour, adding the remaining broth, if necessary. Add the kidney beans, and simmer, uncovered, for about 20 minutes. Ladle in bowls, and serve with rice and desired toppings.

Hearty Ground Elk Soup

1/2 **pound ground elk**
4 14 1/2-**ounce cans chicken broth**
1/2 **cup diced onion**
4 **sliced carrots**
4 **sliced celery stalks**
4 **diced potatoes**
2 14-**ounce cans crushed tomatoes**
2 **cups Miller Lite beer**
8 **ounces pasta (elbow macaroni or orzo)**
1 **tablespoon Italian spices (marjoram, oregano, basil)**

Brown the meat in a Dutch oven. Add the remaining ingredients except pasta. Simmer until the veggies are tender. Bring to a boil, and add the pasta. Cover, and simmer until the pasta is cooked. Serve sprinkled with Parmesan cheese.

Elk Mexican Casserole

1 **pound ground elk**
1 **chopped onion**
3 1/2 **cups canned tomatoes**
2 4-**ounce cans chopped green chilies**
1 10-**ounce bag tortilla chips**
1 **pound grated Monterey Jack cheese**
1 **cup whipping cream mixed with 1 tablespoon vinegar**

Brown the meat and onions in a Dutch oven. Add the tomatoes and green chilies. In a baking pan, make layers of broken tortilla chips, meat mixture, and cheese. Pour soured cream over top. Bake uncovered at 350 degrees for about 30 minutes, or until heated through and bubbly.

Elk Noodle Casserole

1 pound ground elk
1 small onion
1 package egg noodles
2 cans cream of chicken soup
1 can milk
Salt and pepper to taste

Brown the elk, onion, salt, and pepper in a Dutch oven. Cook the noodles according to package directions. Mix all the ingredients together, and cook for about 45 minutes. Check the casserole for seasoning, and serve hot.

Blondie's Beans

$1/2$ pound elk burger
2 cans pork and beans
1 can kidney beans
1 can lima beans
1 teaspoon mustard
$1/4$ cup ketchup
$1/4$ cup molasses

In a Dutch oven, brown the meat. Mix in the remaining ingredients, and cook for about 1 hour, or until desired consistency. Check for seasoning, and serve hot.

Elk Pepper Steak

I pound elk roast, sliced
$^1/_4$ cup oil
I clove garlic, minced
I tablespoon soy sauce
I teaspoon salt
$^1/_2$ cup Miller Lite beer
I cup coarsely chopped green pepper
I tablespoon cornstarch
4 cups cooked rice
I package of Chinese stir-fry veggies

In Dutch oven, brown the elk roast in hot oil; add garlic, and cook until yellow. Add the soy sauce, salt, and beer; cover, and cook for about 15 minutes. Add the pepper, and cook for another 10 minutes. Serve over rice with Chinese stir-fry veggies. Use the cornstarch if needed to thicken.

Sauerbraten

I cooked this in my Dutch oven using a large buffalo roast that was given to me from my friends at Quarry Creek Elk & Bison. Elk roast would work as well.

1 boneless roast, rolled and tied (buffalo or elk)
Bacon fat
1 cup red wine vinegar
1 cup red wine
1 large red onion, sliced in rings
3 bay leaves
6 juniper berries, crushed
Sea salt to taste
1 teaspoon fresh ground black pepper
2 1/2 cups chopped onion
1/2 cup beef stock
1/8 teaspoon ginger, minced
2 tablespoons flour
1 1/2 cups chopped celery
1 1/2 cups chopped baby carrots
1/2 cup gingerbread cookies, crushed
3/4 cup sour cream

In a Dutch oven, sear all sides of the roast in bacon fat. The roast should be brown on all sides but very red in the center. In a saucepan, combine vinegar, wine, red onions, two bay leaves, and juniper berries. Bring to a boil. Let cool. Dress the roast with the mixture, and marinate in the refrigerator overnight, turning periodically. Remove meat from the marinade, pat dry, and season with salt and pepper. Strain the marinade, and reserve, discarding solids. Add all the remaining ingredients to the Dutch oven except the cookies and sour cream, and cook on medium-high heat for about 2 1/2 hours. Remove the meat from the oven, and keep it warm. Skim the surface fat, and reduce the liquid over high heat to about 3 cups. Stir in the crushed cookies until the sauce thickens. Remove from heat, and stir in sour cream. Serve over roast.

Elk and Beer Stew with Root Vegetables

2 pounds elk stew meat, chuck, shoulder, or bottom round
2 bay leaves
1 tablespoon dry thyme
1 tablespoon rosemary
$^1/_4$ cup vegetable oil
2 tablespoons butter
1 cup onion, peeled and diced
$^1/_4$ cup flour
12 ounces dark beer
1 quart hot beef broth
$^1/_2$ cup crushed tomatoes
2 teaspoons salt
2 teaspoons black pepper
$^1/_2$ cup carrots, peeled and diced
$^1/_2$ cup celery, diced
1 cup rutabaga, peeled and diced
1 cup parsnips, diced

Season the meat with salt and pepper. Tie the bay leaves, thyme, and rosemary into a sachet garni in cheesecloth. In a large Dutch oven, combine the oil and butter, and heat until the butter bubbles. Add the meat, and brown on all sides. Remove the meat, and set aside. Then add the onions to the oven, and cook until they are golden in color. Sprinkle the onions with flour, and stir to combine well. Return the meat to the Dutch oven, add the beer, hot broth, herb garni, tomatoes, salt, and pepper. Bring to a boil. Add the carrots, celery, rutabaga, and parsnips, and continue to cook for about 1 hour.

Cousin Rick's Quarry Creek Buffalo Steak and 'Shrooms

I buffalo steak
Flour
$^1/_4$ cup butter
I cup diced yellow onions
I pound mushrooms, sliced
$^1/_2$ teaspoon garlic salt with parsley
$^1/_2$ teaspoon white pepper
8 ounces tomato sauce
I tablespoon Worcestershire sauce
Seasoning salt to taste

Cut the meat into strips, and coat with flour. Sauté in melted butter for about 5 minutes. Add the onions and mushrooms, and cook for about 5 more minutes, or until the onions are tender. Add the remaining ingredients, and stir well. Simmer in the Dutch oven for about 2 hours. Check for seasoning, and serve over cooked wild rice.

Bison Onion Swiss Steak (Fort Madison Rodeo Style)

3 pounds buffalo steak, $^3/_4$ inch thick
$^1/_2$ teaspoon garlic salt
$^1/_4$ teaspoon black pepper
2 packages onion soup mix
2 10-ounce cans tomatoes

Cut the buffalo steak into serving-sized pieces, season with garlic salt and pepper, and place in a Dutch oven. Sprinkle onion soup mix over top, and pour the tomatoes over all. Cover, and cook over a slow fire for about 3 hours, or until the meat is done and tender.

Get-Out-of-Dodge Buffalo Goulash

This is an easy, great-tasting meal.

3 pounds buffalo meat, cubed
2 tablespoons bacon drippings
I teaspoon Accent
I can mushroom soup
Pepper to taste

Brown the meat in bacon drippings in Dutch oven. Add the Accent and soup. Cover, and simmer on low coals for about 1 hour. Pepper to taste, and serve hot. Great over buttermilk biscuits.

Molly's Stew

$1/4$-pound elk steak for each ranch hand
Beef stock
5 pounds potatoes
5 pounds carrots
Salt to taste
Pepper to taste
Bay leaves to taste

In a large Dutch oven, cover the meat with beef stock, and bring to a full boil. Cook for about 30 minutes, covered. Throw in the potatoes and carrots and remaining ingredients. Bring to a boil, and serve after the potatoes and carrots are tender.

Great Buffalo Balls of Fire!

I pound buffalo sausage (hot)
I teaspoon cayenne
I egg
6 ounces grated cheddar cheese
3 cups Bisquick

Mix all the ingredients together using your hands. Pinch off small pieces, and roll into balls. Cook for about 15 minutes in a Dutch oven at 350 degrees. Season with salt and pepper. Note: If too hot, back off on the cayenne.

CABIN EQUIPMENT LIST
Shelter
☐ Reservations confirmed at your cabin, if you are renting
☐ Portable screen room
☐ Portable awning or dining tarp

Bedding
☐ Sleeping bag, appropriate for conditions
☐ Queen size sheet for each bed
☐ Sleeping pad
☐ Pillow with pillowcase

Cooking and Eating
☐ Collapsible fresh jug
☐ Food staples
☐ Coffee and tea
☐ Honey and sugar
☐ Cooking oils
☐ Coolers
☐ Camp stove, Dutch oven, cast-iron pans
☐ Fuel for stove, if needed
☐ Mess kits
☐ Can opener
☐ Metal skewers

Cooking and Eating *continued*
- ☐ Salt, pepper, and spices
- ☐ Pot holder
- ☐ Paper towels
- ☐ Trash bags
- ☐ Cooking utensils, including tongs and spatula
- ☐ Heavy foil
- ☐ Measuring cups
- ☐ Plastic tableware
- ☐ Ziploc bags
- ☐ Knives
- ☐ Small cutting board
- ☐ Cousin Rick's *Cabin Cookin'* cookbook

Cleaning Items
- ☐ Broom
- ☐ Dustpan
- ☐ Whisk broom
- ☐ Rake
- ☐ Dishwashing detergent, low phosphate
- ☐ Pot scrubber or steel wool pads
- ☐ Dish cloths or sponges
- ☐ Towels
- ☐ Laundry detergent, low phosphate
- ☐ Clothes wire and pins
- ☐ Bag for dirty clothing

2

CAST-IRON
COOKIN'

I have found time and time again, when cooking over a cabin fireplace or a campfire, nothing is better than food prepared in a cast-iron pan. It is heavy, so don't plan to use it for backpacking. Cast iron is an ideal heat conductor that is sure to heat evenly and consistently and will last you a lifetime with proper care. I have had my cast-iron skillets for over 30 years, and I can't count the number of meals I have cooked in each of them. A seasoned cast-iron pan will be stick resistant and provide great-tasting meals every time. One tip I want to pass on is that if you need to store your cast-iron pans for long periods of time, coat the pan inside and out with a lightweight food-grade mineral oil. It's cheap and effective. Once you have sealed the pan with mineral oil, no oxygen can reach the seasoning, and it will last for many months. Just another great tip from your old cousin Rick.

Ham and Cheddar Skillet Pie

¹/₂ cup buttermilk baking mix
¹/₄ cup milk
6 eggs
Salt and pepper to taste
I cup smoked ham, fully cooked and diced
¹/₄ cup green bell pepper, cooked, seeded, and chopped
2 scallions, sliced
2 tablespoons butter
I cup shredded cheese

Combine the first three ingredients and salt and pepper to taste in a large bowl. Mix with a fork until all is blended well. Stir in the ham, green peppers, and scallions. Melt the butter in a cast-iron skillet over medium heat until bubbly. Gradually pour the ham mixture into skillet. Cover and cook for about 12 minutes over medium-low heat, until almost set. Sprinkle with cheese. Cover and cook for about 5 more minutes, or until the cheese is melted. Serve hot from skillet.

Fish and Vegetable Skillet Feast

2 carrots, cooked and sliced
¹/₄ cup diced yellow onion
¹/₄ cup water
2 tablespoons dry white wine
¹/₂ teaspoon crushed thyme
³/₄ pound cooked broccoli
I I ounces cream of celery soup
I pound fresh fish fillets, trout if available

Combine the first five ingredients in a well-oiled cast-iron skillet over medium high heat. Season with salt and pepper to taste and bring to a boil. Cover the skillet, reduce the heat to low, and simmer for about 5 minutes, or until the vegetables are just tender. Stir in the broccoli and soup. Raise the heat to medium and bring to a boil.

Arrange the fish in skillet, cover, and reduce the heat to low. Simmer for about 10 minutes, spooning the sauce over fish occasionally. The fish is ready to serve when it flakes apart easily.

Cabin in the Timber Meatballs and Mushrooms

$^1/_3$ **cup breadcrumbs**
I teaspoon dried dill
$^3/_4$ **cup cooked chopped onions**
I egg
I teaspoon Worcestershire sauce
Salt and pepper to taste
12 ounces lean ground beef
2 teaspoons vegetable oil
$^3/_4$ **cup plus 2 tablespoons condensed cream of mushroom soup**
$^1/_3$ **cup skim milk**
I tablespoon plus I teaspoon dry sherry

Combine the breadcrumbs with $^3/_4$ teaspoon dill in a mixing bowl. Stir in the next three ingredients and salt and pepper to taste. Add the meat, and mix with hands until well combined. Form mixture into eight meatballs. Heat oil in skillet over medium heat. Cook the meatballs for about 8 minutes, turning often, until browned all over. Discard any excess fat. Stir in the remaining ingredients and dill. Reduce the heat to low, cover, and simmer for about 8 minutes, or until the meatballs are cooked through.

Cousin Rick's "After the Hunt" Chicken Supper

1 teaspoon salt
1 teaspoon pepper
1 teaspoon paprika
1 teaspoon garlic powder
1 pound large frying chicken, cut into serving pieces
2 teaspoons vegetable oil
2 tablespoons water
1 onion, chopped and cooked
2 potatoes, peeled and cut into French fry–style strips
1 tablespoon slivered almonds
$^1/_2$ pound tomato sauce
1 cup chicken broth
1 teaspoon sugar
10 ounces frozen mixed vegetables
4 whole-wheat dinner rolls

Combine the first four ingredients together, and rub them over the chicken. Heat oil in skillet over medium heat. Cook the chicken, skin side down, for about 6 minutes, or until browned. Add water, cover, and simmer for about 30 minutes, turning chicken every 10 minutes. Transfer the chicken to a platter, and set aside. Add the onion and potatoes, increase heat to medium-high, and sauté for about 3 minutes. Stir in the next four ingredients and bring to a boil, stirring frequently. Stir in vegetables and chicken. Cover, and simmer over medium heat for about 10 minutes, or until the vegetables are tender. Serve with dinner rolls.

Duck-Creek Cabin Skillet Vegetables

2 tablespoons cornstarch
14 ounces chicken stock
1 teaspoon thyme
$^1/_4$ teaspoon pepper
1 pound small red potatoes, cut into quarters
2 cooked carrots, cut into 1-inch pieces
1 cup cooked celery, cut into 2-inch pieces

Combine the cornstarch and $^1/_4$ cup stock in a bowl, and mix until smooth. Set aside. Combine the remaining stock and the next five ingredients in a skillet over medium heat. Bring to a boil. Reduce the heat to low. Cover, and cook for about 20 minutes, or until the vegetables are tender. Remove the vegetables to a serving dish with a slotted spoon. Stir reserved cornstarch mixture, and add to the skillet. Cook until the mixture boils and thickens, stirring constantly. Serve over the vegetables.

Uncle Marvin's Cabin Skillet Meatloaf

1 onion, chopped and cooked
1 green bell pepper, chopped and cooked
$3/4$ cup breadcrumbs
$1/4$ cup skim milk
1 egg
1 teaspoon garlic salt
Pepper
1 pound lean ground beef
2 teaspoons vegetable oil
$1^1/4$ cups tomato sauce
$1/4$ cup ketchup
$1/2$ cup water

Combine the first six ingredients and pepper to taste in a mixing bowl. Add the beef, and knead with your hands until mixed thoroughly. Add oil to skillet. Transfer the meat mixture to the skillet and form into an 8-inch patty. Cover, and cook over medium heat for about 5 minutes, occasionally lifting up patty with a wide spatula and tilting the pan to let oil run underneath, until bottom is browned. Discard excess fat. Place a plate over top of skillet and carefully invert skillet and plate together so patty is on plate. Slide patty, uncooked side down, back into the skillet, and cook about 3 minutes, until underside is just beginning to brown. Discard excess fat. Combine the tomato sauce, ketchup, and water in a bowl. Pour over meat, and bring to a simmer. Reduce the heat to low, cover, and simmer for about 20 minutes until the patty is cooked through. Let stand for 5 minutes before cutting into wedges and serving with sauce from skillet.

Bug-Tussel Scalloped Taters

2 teaspoons butter
1 1/2 pounds potatoes, peeled and thinly sliced
1 red onion, cooked and thinly sliced
1 tablespoon flour
Salt and pepper
2 cups milk

Melt half the butter in a cast-iron skillet over medium heat. Remove from heat, and arrange half of the potatoes in the bottom of the skillet. Cover with onions and sprinkle with half of the flour. Season with salt and pepper to taste. Top with the remaining potato slices, flour, and butter. Pour the milk over the potatoes and bring to a boil over high heat. Cover the pan, reduce the heat, and simmer for about 13 minutes until the potatoes are tender.

Degrange's Cabin Skillet Chops with Rice

4 pork chops
1 cup long-grain white rice
1 1/3 cups chicken stock
1 pound Italian-style peeled tomatoes, chopped
1 leek, cooked and chopped
1/4 cup chopped scallions
1/3 cup golden raisins
1/2 teaspoon rosemary
1 minced garlic clove
Salt and pepper

Heat an oiled cast-iron skillet over high heat, and sauté the pork chops for about 2 minutes per side, or until both sides of chops are browned. Transfer the chops to a platter. Add the remaining ingredients and salt and pepper to taste to skillet, and bring to a boil. Reduce the heat to low. Arrange the pork chops on top of rice, cover, and simmer for about 40 minutes. Check again for seasoning, and serve hot.

Bubba's Beans and Rice Skillet

1 pound ground beef
1 cup water
$^1/_2$ cup thick salsa
15 ounces tomato sauce
1 $^1/_2$ cups uncooked instant white rice
1 cup frozen whole-kernel corn
1 cup chopped red bell pepper
1 15-ounce can black beans, rinsed and drained
Salt and pepper

Brown the beef in a cast-iron skillet over medium heat; add the next three ingredients, and mix well. Bring to a boil. Stir in the remaining ingredients. Reduce the heat to low, cover, and simmer for about 12 minutes, or until the rice is cooked and the vegetables are tender. Salt and pepper to taste, and serve hot from skillet.

Lake Keokuk Cabin Cabbage

2 tablespoons vegetable oil
3 cups finely shredded cabbage
1 cup chopped celery
1 chopped green bell pepper
1 chopped onion
$^1/_2$ teaspoon salt
$^1/_2$ teaspoon pepper

Heat the oil in a cast-iron skillet about 20 minutes before serving time. Add the other ingredients, and cook over medium heat for about 15 minutes, stirring often. Cover the pan during the last 5 minutes of cooking time. Serve the crisp vegetables immediately.

Mrs. Shirley's Ham Skillet Gumbo

2 cups diced cooked ham
I cup chopped green bell pepper
I cup chopped onions
I 10-ounce package frozen cut okra
I 15-ounce can tomatoes
I cup chicken broth
I cup water
I teaspoon salt
$^1/_2$ teaspoon cayenne
I cup uncooked rice

Combine all the ingredients except the rice in a cast-iron skillet, and bring to a boil. Cover the skillet, and simmer on low for about 10 minutes. Stir in the rice, and simmer, covered, for another 20 minutes, or until the rice is tender.

Cajun's in the Cabin Jambalaya

2 cups small shrimp
I cup chopped green bell pepper
I cup chopped onion
I 10-ounce package sliced okra
I 14$^1/_2$-ounce can diced tomatoes
I cup chicken broth
I cup water
I teaspoon salt
I teaspoon pepper
$^1/_2$ teaspoon cayenne
I cup uncooked rice

Combine all the ingredients except rice in a cast-iron skillet; bring to a boil, reduce the heat, cover, and simmer for about 12 minutes. Stir in the rice, and simmer, tightly covered, for about 20 minutes longer, or until the rice is tender.

Hawkeye Cast-Iron Fried Fish

2 pounds fresh fish fillets
Salt and pepper
I egg
I tablespoon milk
I cup dry cornmeal
Fat for cooking
Lemon wedges

Cut the fillets into serving-sized portions. Sprinkle both sides with salt and pepper. Beat the egg slightly, and blend in milk. Dip the fish portions in the egg mixture and then roll them in cornmeal. Place the fish in a cast-iron skillet with about 1/4 inch melted fat, hot but not smoking. Fry at a moderate heat until the fish is brown on one side. Turn carefully and brown the other side. Cooking time is approximately 10 minutes, depending on the thickness of the fish. Drain on absorbent paper, and serve with lemon wedges after checking for seasoning.

Sibs's Chili Pork Chops

6 pork chops
I 10³/4-ounce can condensed tomato soup
I 15-ounce can pinto beans
¹/2 cup sliced onion
I tablespoon chili powder
I minced garlic clove
6 green bell pepper rings

Brown the pork chops in a lightly oiled cast-iron skillet. Pour off any excess fat, and then season the chops with salt and pepper. Add the tomato soup, beans, onion, chili powder, and garlic. Cover the skillet, and cook over low heat for about 15 minutes. Top each chop with a green pepper ring, cover, and cook for 15 minutes longer.

Hayman's Cabin Fried Corn

8 ears of corn
2 tablespoons butter
Salt and pepper

Over a large bowl, cut the kernels from the corn ears. Scrape the cobs to get all the milky liquid. Place the corn and liquid in a cast-iron skillet. Add the butter to the corn, bring the corn mixture to a low boil, and reduce the heat. Cook the corn, stirring constantly, until the juices begin to thicken. Simmer for about 5 minutes, stirring constantly to prevent scorching. Remove from heat, season with salt and pepper, and serve immediately.

Howling Wolf Cube Steak Skillet

4 cube steaks
I teaspoon salt
I teaspoon pepper
Oil
$1/2$ teaspoon garlic powder
10 ounces tomato sauce
15 ounces water
$1/4$ cup chopped cilantro
I tablespoon minced jalapeño peppers

Salt and pepper the steaks to taste, and brown in a cast-iron skillet, using a little oil. Add the remaining ingredients, cover, and simmer for about 20 minutes, or until the sauce has a gravy-like consistency.

Buck Run Skillet Vittles

I pound ground beef
$^1/_2$ cup chopped red onion
$^1/_2$ cup chopped green bell pepper
$^1/_2$ cup chopped cabbage
I cup uncooked long-grain rice
I 15-ounce can tomato sauce
I 6-ounce can tomato paste
2 cups water
I teaspoon salt
$^1/_2$ teaspoon garlic salt
$^1/_2$ teaspoon thyme
I bay leaf

Brown the ground beef in a lightly seasoned cast-iron skillet, stirring to break up. Add the onion, green pepper, cabbage, and rice. Stir in the tomato sauce, tomato paste, water, and seasonings. Bring the mixture to a low boil, and then reduce the heat to a simmer. Cover, and simmer for about 30 minutes, or until the rice is tender, stirring occasionally and adding more water if necessary.

Tyler Cook's Iowa Cabin Catfish

I pound catfish fillets
$^1/_4$ pound butter
I teaspoon garlic powder
I teaspoon dill weed powder
I teaspoon ground dried lemon peel
I teaspoon white pepper

Melt the butter in a cast-iron skillet over medium heat. When melted, add the garlic powder, dill powder, lemon peel, and pepper. Stir well using a large wooden spoon. Pat the catfish fillets dry using paper towels, and place them in the skillet. Using medium heat so the seasonings do not burn, cook for about 5 minutes. Turn the fillets, and cook for about 4 minutes, or until the meat flakes easily with a fork. Serve the fillets with remaining sauce in skillet.

Chippewa Falls Beef and Barley

3/4 pound ground beef
1/2 cup chopped onions
1/4 cup chopped celery
1/4 cup chopped green bell pepper
I teaspoon salt
I teaspoon black pepper
1/2 teaspoon marjoram
I teaspoon sugar
I teaspoon Worcestershire sauce
1/2 cup chili sauce
2 cups canned tomatoes
I cup water
1/2 cup beer
3/4 cup quick-cooking barley

In a seasoned cast-iron skillet, sauté the beef, onion, celery, and green pepper. Drain off excess fat, and stir in the remaining ingredients. Bring to a boil. Reduce the heat to a simmer, cover the skillet, and cook for about 40 minutes. Check the dish for seasonings, and serve hot from skillet.

Maquoketa Caves Squash

6 sliced yellow squash
I chopped onion
I tablespoon bacon drippings
I teaspoon salt
I teaspoon black pepper

In a large cast-iron skillet, melt the bacon drippings, and add the squash slices and onions in layers, sprinkling salt and pepper between the layers. Cover the skillet, and cook over low heat. When the squash starts to become tender, mix gently, and chop the squash to serving-sized pieces. Cook for about 20 minutes, and serve after rechecking the seasoning.

Skillet Sloppy Joes

2 tablespoons butter
I pound ground chuck
$^1/_4$ cup chopped onion
$^1/_2$ teaspoon garlic powder
$^1/_2$ teaspoon salt
$^1/_4$ teaspoon pepper
2 teaspoons dry mustard
I $^1/_2$ teaspoons vinegar
I teaspoon Worcestershire sauce
$^1/_3$ cup Parmesan cheese
I cup frozen corn kernels, cooked

Melt the butter in a seasoned cast-iron skillet. Add the ground chuck, onions, garlic powder, salt, pepper, and dry mustard. Sauté until the meat is no longer pink. Add the vinegar and remaining ingredients. Simmer for about 20 minutes. Serve on split buttered buns that have been toasted.

Mitch King's #47 Sweet Potatoes Skillet

2 teaspoons olive oil
I cup sliced onions
I pound sweet potatoes
$^1/_2$ cup vegetable stock
I teaspoon salt
$^1/_2$ teaspoon pepper

In a large cast-iron skillet, heat the oil, and cook the onions, stirring occasionally, for about 5 minutes or until softened. Meanwhile, peel the potatoes, cut them into $^1/_2$-inch-thick strips, and add to the skillet along with the stock. Cover tightly, and simmer, stirring every 5 minutes, for about 20 minutes, or until the potatoes are tender. Stir in the salt and pepper, and serve hot from skillet.

Cookin' on Olive Court Pork Skillet Supper

2 tablespoons butter
I pound pork tenderloin, cut into $^1/_4$-inch pieces
15 ounces chicken broth
2 teaspoons Worcestershire sauce
$^1/_2$ teaspoon salt
$^1/_2$ teaspoon black pepper
8 quartered red potatoes
I cup sliced mushrooms
$^1/_2$ cup sliced green onions
2 tablespoons flour

Melt the butter in a large cast-iron skillet over medium heat. Add the pork slices; cook for about 5 minutes, or until the meat is browned on both sides. Remove the meat from the skillet; set aside. Reserve $^1/_4$ cup of the chicken broth. Add the remaining chicken broth, Worcestershire sauce, salt, pepper, and potatoes to skillet. Bring to a boil. Reduce the heat to low, cover, and simmer for about 10 minutes, or until the potatoes are tender. Stir in the mushrooms, onions, and pork slices. Cover; simmer an additional 5 minutes, or until the vegetables are tender. In a small bowl, combine the flour and reserved chicken broth; blend it until smooth. Gradually stir into pork mixture. Cook, and stir over medium heat until the mixture is bubbly and thickened. Check for seasoning, and serve hot from skillet.

Rebecca's Ranch Cabin Chicken and Broccoli

I tablespoon butter
4 boneless skinless chicken breast halves
I 10-ounce can broccoli cheese soup
$^1/_2$ cup milk
2 cups broccoli florets
$^1/_2$ cup shredded cheddar cheese
$^1/_2$ teaspoon white pepper

In a large cast-iron skillet, melt the butter until bubbly but not smoking, cook the chicken for about 10 minutes or until browned on both sides. Remove the chicken, and set aside. Spoon off the fat. Combine the remaining ingredients, and bring to a low boil. Return the chicken to the skillet. Cover and simmer for about 15 minutes, or until the chicken is no longer pink and the broccoli is tender and crisp.

Cussing Dale Mizer's Cast-Iron Goulash

I pound lean ground beef
$^1/_2$ cup chopped onion
16 ounces canned tomatoes
$^1/_2$ cup chopped celery
$^1/_2$ cup water
I teaspoon salt
I teaspoon pepper
$^1/_2$ teaspoon basil
$^1/_2$ teaspoon marjoram
I$^1/_2$ cups pasta shells, uncooked

Cook and stir the meat and onion in a large, seasoned cast-iron skillet until the meat is brown and the onions are tender. Drain off any fat. Stir in the tomatoes with liquid and the remaining ingredients, stirring to break up the tomatoes. Heat the mixture to a boil, and then reduce the heat and simmer, covered, stirring every 3 minutes, until the pasta shells are tender, about 20 minutes. Check the goulash for seasoning, and serve hot from skillet.

Snow-Crest Cabin Steak-and-Potato Skillet

1 pound beef round steak, cut into 4 serving-sized pieces
$^1/_4$ cup flour
2 teaspoons vegetable oil
1 cup chopped onion
$^1/_4$ cup chopped green bell pepper
1 16-ounce can small whole potatoes, drained, liquid reserved
$^1/_4$ cup ketchup
2 teaspoons Worcestershire sauce
1 teaspoon beef bouillon granules
1 teaspoon salt
$^1/_2$ teaspoon marjoram
$^1/_4$ teaspoon pepper
2 cups frozen cut green beans

Place the flour in a large plastic bag. Shake each steak in bag to coat with flour, using a meat mallet to pound the flour into the meat. In a large cast-iron skillet, heat the oil over medium heat. Brown the steaks on both sides. Add the onion and green pepper to skillet, and cook until the onion is tender. Drain off fats. To reserved potato liquid, add enough water to make 1 cup. Mix the potato liquid with ketchup, Worcestershire sauce, bouillon, salt, marjoram, and pepper. Pour this onto the beef and onion mixture. Heat the skillet to boiling, reduce the heat, cover, and simmer for about 2 hours. Add the potatoes and green beans, and bring to another boil. Reduce the heat, cover, and simmer for another 15 minutes. Check the dish for seasoning, and serve hot from the skillet.

Pennsylvania Timber Ham-and-Potato Skillet

I tablespoon butter
I pound diced cooked ham
I cup sliced celery
I cup chopped onion
4 cups chopped potatoes
I cup water
$^1/_2$ teaspoon thyme
I teaspoon salt
$^1/_2$ teaspoon pepper
I $^1/_2$ cups frozen cut green beans
$^1/_4$ cup Parmesan cheese

In a large cast-iron skillet, melt the butter until hot and bubbly, and add the ham, celery, and onion. Cook the mixture until the vegetables are tender. Stir in the potatoes, water, thyme, salt, and pepper. Bring to a low boil; reduce the heat. Cover, and simmer on low heat for about 25 minutes. Add the frozen green beans the last 10 minutes of cooking. Top with Parmesan cheese before serving, and recheck for seasoning.

Cabin Critter Cast-Iron Cookies

I cup chopped dates
I cup sugar
3 tablespoons butter
I beaten egg
$^1/_2$ teaspoon vanilla
2 cups crisp rice cereal
$^3/_4$ cup pecans
I cup flaked coconut

Mix the dates, sugar, butter, and egg in a large cast-iron skillet. Melt the mixture over low heat, and cook for about 5 minutes, until the mixture becomes bubbly. Remove from heat; add the vanilla, rice cereal, and pecans. Allow to cool for about 5 minutes. Roll the mixture into small bite-sized balls, and then roll the balls in the coconut.

Skillet Gravy

1 cup self-rising flour
6 ounces evaporated milk
2 tablespoons bacon grease
1 tablespoon fresh ground black pepper
1 teaspoon salt

In a large mixing bowl, combine the flour and milk, and let it sit for about 5 minutes. Heat the bacon grease in a cast-iron skillet, and add the milk mixture. Heat the mixture to a low boil, stirring often. Add the salt and pepper, simmer for about 5 minutes, and serve with biscuits or toast.

HOW TO BUILD A CAMPFIRE

Most cabin rentals will allow you to have your own campfire site. Campfires provide hours of entertainment along with great cooking possibilities. Here are my tips on how to build a campfire.

The very first step before building your campfire should always be to confirm that campfires are allowed in the current conditions.

To begin building a fire, gather the materials, and organize them before striking the first match. Stack your firewood upwind about five feet from where you plan your fire. Clear the area of excess pine needles, dried grasses or leaves, and splash water around the area but not in the planned fire pit or on your building materials.

Create a good foundation by placing rocks in a circle. Lay fine tinder, such as shavings from dried twigs or pine needles, on them. It is best not to use leaves since they float into the air very easily. Perhaps the simplest and most effective approach is to use fire starter. Above the tinder bed, place a few larger dry twigs about the size of a pencil in a crisscross pattern. Have larger pieces of wood at hand. Lay your tinder beside a short length of sticks (about 3 to 6 inches in diameter), and lean the larger twigs over the tinder and against the large stick. Use caution because when the tinder catches, the twigs will flare up quickly. Add one larger piece of wood. This will allow you to add still larger pieces of wood, and you will soon have a good blaze. As the fire subsides, you will have a fine bed of hot coals, and this is the time to really get to some serious cooking!

3

CABIN COOKIN'
WITH FOIL

From the time your old cousin Rick was a Cub Scout, I
fell in love with outdoor cooking. One of the funnest ways to cook
food is with foil. Foil wrap recipes are easy, require few cooking utensils, and leave little to clean up. They can easily feed one person or
a crowd of hungry campers. All you need is some heavy foil and a
charcoal grill or a campfire. Here are some of my favorite recipes for
your enjoyment. This chapter is also a good learning tool to teach
the young the art of outdoor cookery.

Duke's Cabbage and Smoked Sausage Wrap

I head of cabbage, cut into I-inch pieces
I pound smoked sausage, cut into ¹/₄-inch slices
I diced onion
I diced red bell pepper
6 potatoes, cut and quartered into I-inch pieces
2 chopped carrots
I stick butter, chopped
I teaspoon garlic powder
6 slices American cheese
Salt and pepper

Combine all the ingredients together, and wrap in a large sheet of heavy foil that has been coated with cooking oil. Fold to seal all ends. Place on a rack over medium heat or coals for about 35 minutes per side. Salt and pepper to taste, and serve hot.

Jeff May's Cabin Trout

I fresh cleaned trout
I tablespoon butter
¹/₄ teaspoon garlic salt
¹/₄ teaspoon pepper
I slice onion

Clean the fish. Leaving the fish whole, stuff the insides with butter, garlic salt, pepper, and as many onion slices as will fit. Place the stuffed trout on buttered heavy foil, and wrap it tight, sealing all ends. Place the fish over fire for about 10 minutes, turning every 3 minutes. Open the foil pack, peel off the skin, and recheck for seasoning.

Flatheads Burger Wrap

I pound ground beef
$^1/_4$ cup **BBQ sauce (from** *Grillin' Like a Villain* **cookbook)**
$^1/_2$ **cup minced onions**
$^1/_2$ **cup sliced potatoes**
$^1/_2$ **cup chopped carrots**
I **teaspoon salt**
I **teaspoon pepper**

Lay out a large piece of heavy foil. Shape the ground beef into a large thick patty. Make a well in the center of the patty. Place the patty in the center of the foil. Spoon the BBQ sauce into the burger well. Add the remaining ingredients into the well. Wrap the patty in the foil, sealing all ends tightly. Cook the burger over hot coals or grate for about 12 minutes per side, or until the meat is no longer pink and the vegetables are the desired tenderness.

Onion-Wrapped Taters

4 **large potatoes**
I **12-ounce package dry onion soup mix**
I **stick butter, sliced**
I **teaspoon Accent**
I **teaspoon pepper**

Wash, peel, and thinly slice the potatoes. Put a layer of potato slices on a large piece of heavy foil, top with butter slices and half of the soup mix. Layer again with the remaining ingredients. Seal the potatoes tightly, and cook on coals for about 15 minutes per side. Season cooked potatoes with Accent and pepper to taste.

"My Mouth's on Fire Momma!" Chicken Wrap

I chicken breast with bone and skin
3 hot banana peppers in vinegar
I large potato
I carrot
I zucchini
$1/4$ teaspoon cayenne
$1/4$ teaspoon seasoning salt
$1/4$ teaspoon chili powder

Wash and thinly slice the vegetables. Place all ingredients in a buttered foil pouch, and let cook by the fire coals for about 12 minutes per side. The chicken is done when the juices are clear and the veggies are tender. Check for seasoning. Note: This is a very hot dish.

Hamster Wraps

I cup cooked diced ham
I large onion
I cup canned sweet corn
I cup canned green beans
I teaspoon season salt
$1/2$ teaspoon garlic powder
2 tablespoons soft butter

Cut the onion in slices, and pull apart. Mix all the ingredients together. Divide into five sheets of heavy foil. Fold up each foil packet, and tightly seal all. Cook for about 12 minutes per side on grill or over campfire. Check for seasoning, and serve hot from foil packets.

Tomcat Cabin Casserole

4 large potatoes, sliced
1 bag frozen mixed vegetables
2 pounds lean hamburger, uncooked
1 chopped yellow onion
2 cups canned mushroom soup
Salt and pepper

Layer the ingredients in order into a foil roasting pan. Break up the hamburger and spread it evenly over the vegetables. Cover the pan with heavy foil. Cook over hot fire coals for about 60 minutes. Season to taste with salt and pepper before serving.

Campfired Baked Potato

1 large baking potato
1 small sliced yellow onion
1 teaspoon butter
1 tablespoon real bacon bits
$1/4$ teaspoon garlic salt

Slice the potato, and add the onion slices between the potato slices. Lay butter and bacon bits on top so the butter can melt over the potato slices while cooking. Season the potato slices with garlic salt to taste. Wrap all in heavy foil, and lay in a bed of campfire coals. Rotate every 2 minutes for a total of about 10 minutes cooking time.

Wings of Paradise

20 chicken wings
Dry BBQ seasoning to taste

Fold the foil to make a large pocket for the fire grate. Place the wings on the foil, and sprinkle with BBQ seasoning. Cover with foil, and cook for about 60 minutes, or until the chicken is done and tender. Check the wings for seasoning, and serve hot while watching the campfire.

Campfire Crappie

4 crappie fillets
I tablespoon butter
I dash lemon pepper
I dash garlic powder
I dash salt

Place the fillets in foil, seasoning with butter, and seal tightly. Place the foil pack near the campfire, and cook for about 10 minutes per side. Check the fish for seasoning, and serve hot from foil packets.

Campfire Ham

I medium-sized boneless ham
3 cloves
$^1/_2$ cup crushed pineapple, with juice
$^1/_2$ cup sliced pineapple, with juice
I cup brown sugar

Slice the ham into serving-sized pieces. Add the ham slices, cloves, pineapple and juices, and brown sugar to a foil roasting pan, and cover with foil. Cook the ham on rack over campfire, being careful to set it to the side of the fire. Cook ham for about 60 minutes. Check the meat for seasoning, and serve from foil pan.

Cabin Times Meatloaf Wrap

2 pounds ground beef
I egg
$^1/_2$ cup seasoned breadcrumbs
$^1/_2$ cup tomato soup
Garlic salt and pepper

Lay out a large sheet of heavy foil. Place the ground beef in the middle of the foil, and make a well in the middle of beef. Add the remaining ingredients, and mix well. Shape the meat into a loaf. Wrap the loaf well with the foil, leaving room for steam. Cook for about 45 minutes over a campfire grate, turning the loaf every 15 minutes. Check the loaf for seasoning before serving.

Chirping Crickets Pork Tenderloin

I pork tenderloin
2 tablespoons olive oil
2 thinly sliced apples
$^1/_2$ cup sliced onion
I tablespoon teriyaki sauce

Make a large pocket out of heavy foil. Rub all sides of the pork tenderloin with olive oil. Place the loin and the remaining ingredients into foil pocket, and seal tightly. Grill each of the four sides of the pocket for about 15 minutes per side. The meat is ready for serving when the juices are clear and the apples are tender. Check the meat for seasoning, and serve hot.

Huck Finn Foiled Supper

I pound stew meat
$^1/_2$ cup canned corn
$^1/_4$ cup canned green beans
$^1/_4$ cup canned carrots
$^1/_4$ cup sliced onion
I minced garlic clove
Salt and pepper
$^1/_2$ stick chopped butter

Tear off a piece of heavy foil large enough to fold into a pocket for your ingredients. Spray the foil with cooking spray. Add the meat first and then the vegetables. Top with seasonings and then butter. Close foil on all sides, leaving room for steam to build. Put the packet into the coals. Cooking time depends on how hot your fire is. Check and turn packet every 10 minutes until the meat and vegetables are done and tender.

Tasty Olive Chicken

4 boneless, skinless chicken breast halves
I thinly sliced onion
2 cups canned diced tomatoes with garlic and onions, drained
I cup canned sliced ripe olives, drained
$^1/_2$ cup shredded Parmesan cheese

In a large strip of foil that has been coated with cooking oil, place all the ingredients together except the cheese, and season to taste. Carefully bring up the foil sides, and double-fold the top and ends to seal the packet, leaving room for the heat to circulate inside. Grill for about 25 minutes, turning the packet twice. Sprinkle with cheese before serving.

Kidder's Timber Chicken Packet

4 chicken breast halves
4 tablespoons Dijon mustard
2 tablespoons basil
2 tablespoons paprika
2 carrots, cut into strips
2 cups sliced mushrooms
2 sliced zucchini
Salt and pepper

Coat the chicken breast with Dijon mustard. Place the coated meat and the remaining ingredients on a large sheet of heavy foil that has been coated with cooking oil. Bring up the foil sides, and double-fold the top ends to seal the packet, leaving room for heat to circulate inside the packet. Grill the meat packet on a campfire grate for about 25 minutes, turning twice. The meat is done when the juices are clear.

Spam-O-Licious

This cabin recipe was first introduced to me in the spring of 2001, while fishing in Canada. Larry (Chopper) Krueger was the guide who made this dish.

I can of Spam luncheon meat, cut ¼-inch slices
I can crushed pineapple
I can potatoes
I can yams
I tablespoon butter
I cup brown sugar

In a large, doubled piece of heavy foil, layer the Spam slices. Cover them with the potatoes and yams. Layer with ½ cup of brown sugar and the pineapples. Layer again with remaining brown sugar and butter. Fold the foil from top until it is tight around the ingredients of the packet. Do the same with the ends of the foil. Place the packet on hot coals, and cook for about 10 minutes. Turn over, and cook for another 10 minutes.

Travis's (My Boy) Garlic Cod

4 Alaskan cod fillets (caught by the old man)
$^1/_4$ cup soy sauce
2 teaspoons sesame oil
2 minced garlic cloves
$^1/_2$ teaspoon red pepper flakes
3 cups fresh snow peas
2 cups sliced mushrooms
2 sliced carrots
1 tablespoon toasted sesame seeds

Cut out four large strips of heavy foil, and spray the centers of the sheets with cooking spray. Place one cod fillet on each piece. Combine the soy sauce, oil, garlic, and red pepper flakes; spoon 1 teaspoon over each fillet. Top with the vegetables. Spoon remaining sauce over vegetables. Double-fold the top and ends to seal the packet, leaving room for heat to circulate inside. Repeat this on all four packets. Place near fire for 20 minutes, turning twice, or on grill for about 12 minutes, covered. Sprinkle with the sesame seeds before serving.

Coon Hunters Foiled Ham Supper

³/₄ pound ham, cut into cubes
2 cups cooked rice
I cup canned black-eyed peas, drained
I cup canned diced tomatoes
I teaspoon minced garlic
I tablespoon minced onion
I teaspoon Louisiana hot sauce
I chopped green bell pepper
Salt and pepper

Cut out four large strips of heavy foil, and spray the centers of the sheets with cooking spray. Combine the ham, rice, peas, tomatoes, garlic, onion, hot sauce, and green bell pepper. Check for seasoning, and place one-fourth of the mixture on each sheet of foil. Bring up the sides, and double-fold the top and ends to seal. Repeat this on the remaining three sheets of foil. Place the foil packets on a covered grill or campfire grate, and cook for about 15 minutes, turning once.

Camp El-Keota Cabin Loin

1 yellow onion, cut into rings
1 pound pork tenderloin, sliced
1 pound squash, peeled and sliced
1 teaspoon dried rosemary
$^1/_2$ cup maple syrup
2 tablespoons balsamic vinegar
1 tablespoon cornstarch
$^1/_2$ cup sweetened cranberries
Salt and pepper

Cut two doubled sheets of heavy foil, and spray the centers of the sheets with cooking spray. Place half the onion on each sheet of foil, and top both with the pork loin slices. Place the squash around the pork slices. Sprinkle with the rosemary. In a bowl, combine the syrup, vinegar, and cornstarch; spoon over the pork. Sprinkle with the cranberries, and season all with salt and pepper. Bring up the foil sides, and double-fold the tops and ends to seal the packet. Cook on a covered grill or campfire grate for about 15 minutes, or until all is done and tender.

Skokie's Cabin Meal

1 pound smoked sliced turkey sausage
1 pound sliced red potatoes
1 chopped green bell pepper
1 cup garlic spaghetti sauce
$^1/_2$ teaspoon garlic salt
$^1/_2$ teaspoon pepper

Cut out two large sheets of heavy foil, and spray the centers with cooking oil. Combine all the ingredients, and place half of the mixture on each sheet of foil. Bring up the sides, and double-fold the tops and ends to seal the foil packets. Cook on campfire grate for about 30 minutes, turning twice.

Mike Black's Cabin on the Gulf Shrimp

4 pounds large shrimp
I cup butter
I minced garlic clove
$^1/_2$ teaspoon black pepper
I teaspoon salt
I cup minced parsley

Peel and clean the shrimp. Cream butter; add the remaining ingredients to the butter and mix well. Cut six 9-inch strips of heavy foil, and then cut each strip in half. Divide the shrimp equally on each piece of foil. Top each with the butter mixture, bring the foil up around shrimp, and twist tightly to seal. Place the shrimp packets on hot embers, and cook for about 5 minutes.

Billy's Banana Boat

I banana
12 small marshmallows
$^1/_4$ cup chocolate chips

Peel back a long strip of banana peel on the inside of the curve, leaving one end attached to the banana. Scoop out some of the banana and fill with marshmallow and chocolate chips. Replace the strip of peeling and wrap with foil. Cook the banana packet on hot embers for about 20 minutes, or until the banana, chocolate chips, and marshmallows are melted and blended well.

Cousin Rick's Dry-Rub T-Bone

I teaspoon garlic powder
I teaspoon paprika
I teaspoon brown sugar
I teaspoon salt
I teaspoon pepper
I teaspoon cayenne
I large T-bone steak

Cut out a large strip of heavy foil, and spray the inside of the foil with cooking oil. In a small bowl, combine the garlic powder, paprika, brown sugar, salt, pepper, and cayenne. Mix the ingredients well. Rub the steak on all sides, using your fingers to work in the rub. Wrap the steak with the foil, and cook for about 20 minutes on a campfire grill grate, turning twice.

Timberline Brisket

I small beef brisket
$^1/_2$ cup water
I tablespoon flour
$^1/_2$ teaspoon garlic salt
$^1/_2$ teaspoon pepper
I yellow onion, sliced into rings

Using a very large sheet of heavy foil, make a pouch large enough to hold the brisket inside, leaving room to fold and seal. Lightly spray the inside of the pouch with cooking spray. Combine the water and flour; pour into pouch. Generously sprinkle the brisket with the garlic salt and pepper; place into the pouch. Arrange the onion rings on top of the brisket. Double-fold the open end of the pouch to seal. Cook on grill or campfire grate for about 2 hours, turning every 30 minutes, or until the brisket is your desired tenderness.

Squirrel Bark Cabin Apples

12 apples
4 tablespoons sugar
³/4 cup biscuit mix
¹/4 cup raisins
3 tablespoons cinnamon

Core and chop apples in large pieces. Mix 1 teaspoon sugar, a few raisins, and cinnamon to taste with 1 tablespoon biscuit mix; stir into chopped apple. Wrap the apple mix in a piece of greased foil, leaving space for steam. Do this for each apple. Cook the apples in hot embers for about 40 minutes.

Silver Springs Cabin Baked Apples

12 ripe apples
1 cup nuts
1 cup shredded coconut
12 dates
1 cup brown sugar
12 large marshmallows

Remove the core from each apple. Be sure not to cut through the skin at one end. Fill the hole with nuts, dates, and coconut. Sprinkle well with brown sugar, wrap each apple with foil, and place in hot coals. When tender, toast the marshmallows, and place one on each apple top. Serve hot.

GREAT HERBS FOR COOKIN' VITTLES AT THE CABIN

The following list will give you a basic idea of how to use various herbs with a variety of foods. As always, feel free to experiment with the different flavors to enhance your meals. As a rule of thumb, I recommend you use a small amount of herbs until you know if you like the taste. Never use too many herbs at once. I say, keep it simple until you are familiar with the various flavors, and last but not least, never let your herbs get old and stale.

Basil: Use with eggs, fish, cheese, meatloaf, hash, meat pie, stews, venison, duck, tomatoes, tomato soup, and spaghetti sauces.

Bay Leaf: Use with meat pie, stews, soups, and roast.

Chives: Use with cream, cottage cheese, eggs, fish, potatoes, peas, and carrots.

Dill: Use with pickles, fish sauces, cheese dishes, and salads.

Marjoram: Use with pork, lamb, meatloaf, hash, meat pie, soups, and stews.

Mint: Use with lamb and desserts.

Oregano: Use with spaghetti sauces, tomato sauces, minestrone, pizza, potatoes, and salads.

Parsley: Garnish for eggs, meat, fish, and salad. When chopped or minced is great with soups and stews.

Rosemary: Use with chicken, fish, lamb, pork, meat pie, and in salads.

Sage: Use in sausages and most pork dishes, also great in stuffing.

Savory: A lot like sage but more delicate, great with omelets and salads.

Tarragon: Use with eggs, fish, chicken, and veal.

Thyme: Use with fish, chowder, oyster, clam bisque, meatloaf, hash, meat pie, soups, stews, chicken, turkey, and salads.

Remember that fresh herbs may be used as sprigs or chopped fine. Dry herbs are at least three times as strong as fresh herbs, so measure accordingly. To bring out the flavor of dry herbs, soak them in lemon juice or wine before using them.

4

CABIN SOUPS
AND
STEWS

Eating is fun and so is fixing food to eat. There are so
many opportunities around the cabin and cabin campsite to cook
and eat, and there is just something about cabin and cabin campsite
cooking that is special. Whatever type of cooking you do at your
cabin and methods you have available can make for a challenge
until you become an old pro and master cooking indoors and out. I
will cover all methods of cooking soups and stews in this chapter.
Soups and stews are very popular amongst us cabin folks. Be sure to
try each and every recipe in this chapter, and don't be afraid to
adapt your own seasonings to each recipe—after all, that's what
makes cooking fun! All the following recipes can be prepared with
the following heat sources: Dutch oven, campfire grate, L. P. stove,
and woodstove. Take note that if the recipe calls for a boil, you must
have the heat source that is capable of producing high rapid heat.

Gallows's Ridge Hamburger Stew

2 pounds ground beef
2 cups canned tomato soup
2 cups canned sliced mushrooms, with liquid
2 cups pork and beans
1 cup canned kidney beans, with liquid
1 chopped onion
3 chopped carrots
1 pound potatoes, peeled and cubed
Garlic salt and pepper to taste

Brown the beef and onion in a large pot or kettle, and drain off excess fat. Add the remaining ingredients, and simmer until the potatoes and carrots are tender. Check for seasonings, and serve hot from the pot.

Chow Boss Chowder

6 slices bacon, chopped
2 crushed garlic cloves
2 tablespoons chopped scallions
4 tablespoons flour
5 cups milk
2 cups water
2 chicken stock cubes
3 large cubed potatoes
2 cups canned corn, drained
1/2 cup cream
Salt and pepper

Using a large pot or kettle, brown the bacon, garlic, and scallions in butter until all is tender. Blend the flour with 1 cup milk, and stir into the pot. Simmer until mixture is thick and bubbly. Gradually stir in the remaining ingredients, and simmer, turning often until the potatoes are tender.

Tinker's Cabin Beer Soup

1 cup beer
2 whole cloves
1 tablespoon sugar
$1/4$ teaspoon cinnamon
$1/2$ teaspoon lemon rind
1 cup milk
1 tablespoon flour
1 teaspoon seasoned salt
1 egg yolk

In a medium-sized pot, bring beer to a boil. Add cloves, sugar, cinnamon, and lemon rind. In another pan bring the milk to a boil, and add the flour and seasoned salt. Then add this mixture to the beer. Add the egg yolk, and stir on very low heat for about 5 minutes. Check the soup for seasoning, and serve hot.

Tree Haulers' Cabin Bean Soup

Serves about 50 lumberjacks

5 pounds white beans, soaked overnight
3 cups chopped onions
4 bay leaves
6 minced garlic cloves
2 meaty ham bones
4 cups cubed smoked ham
1 quart mashed potatoes
1 quart chopped celery
1 quart diced carrots

In a very large cast-iron pot or kettle, cover the beans in water, and bring the beans, onion, bay leaves, garlic, ham bones, and ham meat to a rapid boil. Reduce heat, cover, and simmer for about 3 hours, or until the beans are tender. Add the mashed potatoes, celery, and carrots. Season to taste with salt and pepper, and let the soup simmer for another 2 hours. Remove the ham bones, cut off and dice any remaining meat, and add to the soup. Simmer for another 45 minutes, and serve.

Officers' Mess Cabin Corn Soup

Serves about 40

2 pounds butter
2 cups flour
3 tablespoons salt
7 quarts milk
8 cups cream-style corn
3 quarts water
1 chopped yellow onion
1 tablespoon pepper
1 tablespoon paprika
$^1/_2$ cup chopped parsley

In a large soup pot, melt the butter, blend in the flour, and add the salt. Slowly pour in the milk, and stir until the mixture thickens. The white sauce should cook for about 5 minutes with constant stirring after it reaches the boiling point. In a separate pot, boil the corn in water with the onions, pepper, and paprika for about 15 minutes. Add the white sauce mixture, and cook together for about 30 minutes. Add the parsley, and simmer on low heat until ready to serve.

Shaky Pistols Catfish Soup

2 tablespoons peanut oil
I cup sliced onion
2 minced garlic cloves
I teaspoon minced ginger
I chopped catfish fillet
3 cups chicken broth
2 tablespoons plum sauce
2 teaspoons oyster sauce
2 cups cooked rice
I large sliced green onion

In a medium pot or kettle, heat oil. Add the onion and stir-fry until the onion is transparent. Add the garlic and ginger, and stir-fry for another 30 seconds. Place the catfish pieces in pot; reduce the heat, and cook, stirring occasionally so that the fish doesn't stick to the pot. Add the chicken broth, plum sauce, and oyster sauce, and bring to a boil. Add the remaining ingredients, cover, reduce the heat, and simmer on low for about 10 minutes. Check the soup for seasoning, and serve hot from the pot.

Fort Madison Apple Cider Stew

3 tablespoons flour
2 tablespoons salt
I teaspoon black pepper
I teaspoon thyme
3 pounds lamb stew meat
3 tablespoons olive oil
2 cups apple cider
4 cups water
2 tablespoons cider vinegar
I ground bay leaf
5 chopped carrots
4 sliced potatoes
2 chopped onions
2 chopped celery stalks
I chopped apple

Combine the flour, salt, pepper, and thyme in a large mixing bowl. Toss the stew meat into the flour mixture, and mix well. Brown the stew meat with olive oil in a Dutch oven. Stir in the cider, water, and vinegar. Bring the mixture to a boil. Add the bay leaf, and simmer until the stew meat is tender. Add the remaining ingredients, and simmer until the vegetables are tender. Check the stew for seasoning, and serve hot from the Dutch oven.

Beaver Trail Bean Soup

2 tablespoons olive oil
I cup chopped onion
$^1/_2$ cup chopped green bell pepper
$^1/_2$ cup dry red wine
I cup canned diced tomatoes
I cup canned black beans, drained
I cup canned red kidney beans, drained
I cup canned pinto beans, drained
4 teaspoons chili powder
I teaspoon garlic powder
I teaspoon cumin
I teaspoon basil
2 teaspoons sugar
I teaspoon salt
I teaspoon pepper

Heat the olive oil in a large pot or kettle over high heat. Add the onion and green pepper, cook for about 5 minutes, or until the veggies are tender. Stir in the remaining ingredients, and bring to a boil. Reduce the heat, and simmer for about 30 minutes. Check the soup for seasoning, and serve hot.

Chopper's Cabin Camp Chicken Stew

2 cups cream of mushroom condensed soup
$^1/_2$ cup water
2 cups canned mixed vegetables, with liquid
2 cups canned potatoes, with liquid
2 boneless chicken breasts, cut into cubes
I teaspoon parsley
I teaspoon garlic powder
I teaspoon pepper

Add all the ingredients to a large kettle or pot, and cook for about 30 minutes over an open flame, stirring often. Check the stew for seasoning before serving hot.

Birds Be A-Chirpin' Chili Mac

1 pound ground beef
$1/2$ cup chopped green bell pepper
$1/4$ cup chopped onion
1 minced garlic clove
1 cup canned diced tomatoes, with liquid
1 cup tomato sauce
$3/4$ cup uncooked elbow macaroni
$3/4$ cup water
1 packet taco seasoning mix
$1/2$ teaspoon salt
$1/2$ cup Colby Jack cheese

In a large saucepan or pot, brown the beef, green pepper, onion, and garlic for about 10 minutes, or until the beef is no longer pink, breaking beef into crumbles. Drain off fat. Stir in the remaining ingredients, and bring to a boil. Reduce the heat, cover, and simmer for about 20 minutes, stirring often. Remove from heat, and let stand for 5 minutes. Top with grated Colby Jack cheese.

Forest Ranger Chili

3 pounds lean beef, sliced into thin strips
2 tablespoons onion powder
1 tablespoon garlic powder
2 cups tomato sauce
6 tablespoons chili powder
2 tablespoons cumin
1 tablespoon paprika
$1/4$ teaspoon oregano
1 teaspoon cayenne
$1/2$ teaspoon white pepper
1 teaspoon Accent
2 cups beer
1 cup beef broth

Sear the beef in a large heavy pot. Add the remaining ingredients, and simmer on low heat for about 3 hours, stirring often, adding more broth if needed. Check for seasoning, and serve hot.

Western Pines BBQ Beef and Beans

2 pounds round tip roast, sliced into cubes
3 cups chopped onion
3 minced garlic cloves
2 tablespoons vegetable oil
2 tablespoons chili powder
2 tablespoons cumin
$^1/_4$ teaspoon cloves
1 teaspoon garlic salt
$^1/_2$ teaspoon pepper
64 ounces canned chopped tomatoes, with juice
48 ounces canned pinto beans, drained
3 cups beef stock
$^1/_4$ cup molasses
1 tablespoon Louisiana hot sauce
2 teaspoons cider vinegar

Brown the beef, onion, and garlic in oil in a Dutch oven over medium heat until the beef is no longer pink. Stir in the chili powder, cumin, cloves, salt, and pepper. Add the tomatoes, beans, stock, molasses, and Louisiana hot sauce. Simmer over low heat for about 2 hours, stirring every 5 minutes. Stir in the vinegar, check for seasoning, and serve.

Pikes Peak Steer Chowder

$^1/_2$ **cup butter**
$^1/_2$ **cup chopped onion**
$^1/_2$ **cup chopped celery**
16 ounces frozen corn kernels, thawed
32 ounces chicken broth
14 ounces canned, chopped green chilies
1 tablespoon thyme
$^1/_2$ **cup roasted red bell peppers, chopped**
1 pound fully cooked beef roast, shredded
2 cups milk

Melt the butter in a large iron skillet. Sauté the onions, celery, and corn until all are crisp and tender. Combine the chicken broth, chilies, and thyme in a large saucepan, and heat over medium flame until the mixture begins to simmer. Add the cooked vegetables, roasted red peppers, and shredded beef. Add the milk, and heat until warm. Do not allow the chowder to boil. Check for seasoning, and serve hot.

Archie McKensington's Cabin Lamb Stew

3 pounds lamb shoulder, cut into 3-inch pieces
Salt and pepper
2 onions, cut into rings
3 diced carrots
2 diced turnips
2 chopped celery stalks
1 diced cabbage
5 diced potatoes
4 minced garlic cloves
2 teaspoons marjoram

Place the lamb meat into a large heavy pot or kettle, and cover with water. Season with salt and pepper, cover, and simmer for about 45 minutes. Add the remaining ingredients, and simmer for another 45 minutes while covered. Check again for seasoning, and serve.

Lake Stevenson's Hot Dog Soup

1 teaspoon garlic salt
1 teaspoon pepper
1 teaspoon onion powder
2 cups flour
2 quarts water
6 hot dogs
2 eggs
3 cups diced potatoes

Mix the garlic salt, pepper, and onion powder with the flour. Place a large heavy skillet on fire grate, and add 2 quarts of water and diced hot dogs, bringing to a boil. Mix the eggs with the seasoned flour and blend until the mixture becomes sticky. Spoon marble-sized pieces of flour mixture into the boiling water with hot dogs. Add the diced potatoes, and simmer for 2 hours. Season to taste with salt and pepper, and serve.

Sibs's Beef Stew

5 pounds lean cubed beef
4 tablespoons vegetable oil
2 chopped garlic cloves
4 cups hot water
8 cups canned tomatoes
4 chopped white onions
2 tablespoons salt
1 teaspoon pepper
6 tablespoons sugar
12 carrots, peeled and chopped
10 potatoes, quartered
$^1/_2$ teaspoon cloves
$^1/_2$ teaspoon basil
2 cups English peas

In a large skillet, brown the beef in oil. Transfer the cooked beef to a large Dutch oven, and mix in the garlic. Add the water, tomatoes, onions, salt, pepper, and sugar. Mix well, and simmer for about 2 hours, stirring often. Add the carrots, potatoes, cloves, and basil. Cover and cook until the vegetables are tender. Add the peas and simmer. To thicken, add flour dissolved in water, and stir. Check for seasoning, and serve hot.

Green Island Duck Hunting Cabin Stew

2 pounds smoked sausage
4 cups canned green beans, with liquid
10 russet potatoes
Salt and pepper to taste

In a large pot, dump in the green beans with liquid. Slice the smoked sausage, and layer on top of green beans. Chop the potatoes into small pieces, and place on top of the sausage. Cook over medium heat for about 35 minutes, or until the potatoes are tender. Check the soup for seasoning, and serve hot.

Midwest Fall Camp Chili

3 pounds lean ground beef

1 chopped onion

2 chopped green bell peppers

1 minced garlic clove

1 cup whole-kernel corn, drained

1 16-ounce can chili with beans

8 cups vegetable juice

3 tablespoons chili powder

1 cup beer

1 teaspoon salt

1 teaspoon pepper

1 teaspoon oregano

1/2 teaspoon cumin

In a large pot or kettle, brown the beef, onions, peppers, and garlic until the beef is no longer pink and the vegetables are tender. Add the remaining ingredients, and simmer on low for about 4 hours. Check for seasoning, and serve hot.

Sudbeck's Log Cabin Stew

5 pounds chuck steak, cubed into bite-sized pieces

1 pound diced carrots

2 pounds potatoes, quartered

2 chopped yellow onions

4 chopped celery stalks

8 cups tomato sauce

1 cup beef stock

5 beef bouillon cubes

Salt and pepper

In a large stockpot or kettle, brown the chuck steak cubes. Add the remaining ingredients, and check for seasoning. Simmer on low heat for about 4 hours, adding more stock or water if needed. Check again for seasoning, and serve hot, making sure all the vegetables are tender.

Foggy Top Mountain Cabin Cream of Mushroom Soup

14 ounces canned mushrooms, drained, liquid reserved
1 cup water
$^1/_4$ cup butter
2 tablespoons chopped onion
$^1/_4$ cup flour
1 teaspoon seasoned salt
$^1/_2$ teaspoon pepper
12 ounces evaporated milk

Chop the mushrooms, and place in a bowl with reserved mushroom liquid and 1 cup water. Melt the butter in a large saucepan over medium heat. Add the onion, and cook until tender. Remove from heat. Stir in the flour and seasoned salt; return to heat. Stir in the remaining ingredients, and bring to a low boil. Reduce the heat, and simmer for about 5 minutes, stirring constantly, checking for seasoning and serving hot.

Fish Cop Potato and Ham Soup

2 cups red potatoes, peeled and cubed
4 tablespoons butter
1 cup minced onion
3 tablespoons flour
$^1/_2$ teaspoon cayenne
$^1/_2$ teaspoon pepper
3 cups milk
1 teaspoon garlic salt
1 cup cubed ham, cooked
1 cup shredded cheddar cheese
$^1/_4$ cup chopped chives

Cook the potatoes in boiling water until tender. Drain; reserve 1 cup of the liquid. Melt the butter in a large saucepan over medium heat. Add the onion, and cook until tender. Stir in the flour; season with cayenne and black pepper. Cook for about 3 minutes, stirring often. Add the potatoes, reserved liquid, milk, and garlic salt; stir well. Add the ham, and simmer for another 5 minutes, stirring often. Remove from heat, and allow the soup to cool for about 5 minutes. Add the cheese, and stir until melted. Top the soup with the chopped chives, and serve hot.

Uncle Ronnie's Camper Fish Stew

6 tablespoons olive oil
1 cup chopped onion
2 chopped garlic cloves
$^2/_3$ cup chopped parsley
1 cup chopped tomatoes
2 teaspoons tomato paste
8 ounces clam juice
$^2/_3$ cup white wine
2 pounds crappie fillets, chopped
$^1/_4$ teaspoon oregano
$^1/_4$ teaspoon Louisiana hot sauce
$^1/_4$ teaspoon thyme
$^1/_4$ teaspoon white pepper

Heat the olive oil in a large pot or kettle over medium heat. Add the chopped onion and garlic, and sauté for about 5 minutes. Add the parsley, and stir for about 2 minutes. Add the tomatoes and tomato paste, and cook for another 2 minutes longer. Add the clam juice, wine, and fish. Simmer the ingredients until the fish is cooked through. Add the seasonings, and serve hot.

Valley Ridge Veal Stew

2 pounds cubed veal
1 tablespoon olive oil
1 cup chopped onion
2 cups water
$^1/_2$ cup green olives, chopped
2 sprigs thyme
$^1/_2$ teaspoon seasoning salt
$^1/_2$ teaspoon black pepper
12 ounces cream of mushroom soup

Brown the meat in olive oil. Remove the meat, and sauté the onions until they are tender. Place the water, olives, thyme, seasoned salt, and pepper in pot. Add the meat. Simmer on low heat for about 60 minutes. Add the soup, and simmer on low for another 15 minutes, stirring often. Check the soup for seasoning, and serve hot.

Springtime Cabin Jambalaya

2 tablespoons olive oil
1 chopped onion
2 chopped celery stalks
1 chopped green bell pepper
2 minced garlic cloves
1 pound smoked sausage, sliced
2 cups canned black-eyed peas, with liquid
1 14-ounce can diced tomatoes
1 14-ounce can diced tomatoes with green chilies
1 tablespoon Worcestershire sauce
4 cups cooked rice, hot

Sauté the vegetables in the olive oil in a deep skillet. When the vegetables are just tender, add the smoked sausage slices, black-eyed peas with liquid, tomatoes, and Worcestershire sauce. Let the soup simmer for about 25 minutes. Check for seasoning, and serve over hot cooked rice.

Fall Hunt Sweet Corn Soup

1 quart vegetable stock
$^1/_2$ cup ribbon noodles, broken
2 cups sweet corn kernels
$^1/_2$ cup chopped celery
$^1/_2$ teaspoon turmeric
1 teaspoon salt
1 teaspoon pepper

In a large pot, bring the stock to a boil. Add the noodles and sweet corn, and boil for about 6 minutes. Add the celery and turmeric. Stir well, reduce the heat, and simmer for about 15 minutes. Check the soup for seasoning, and serve hot.

Ice Fishin' Soup

2 pounds ground beef
1 chopped onion
6 cups water
10 beef bouillon cubes
6 cups canned diced tomatoes, with liquid
2 cups cooked rice
2 teaspoons salt
1 teaspoon white pepper
$^1/_2$ teaspoon paprika
2 chopped green bell peppers
1 chopped yellow bell pepper

In a large pot, cook the ground beef with onion until the meat is brown and the onion is tender; drain. Add the bouillon cubes, tomatoes, rice, and seasonings. Bring the soup to a boil, reduce the heat, and simmer, covered, for about 65 minutes. Add the chopped peppers, and cook, uncovered, for about 20 minutes. Check the soup for seasoning, and serve hot.

Danny Roberts's Old Thrashers' Split Pea Soup

2 cups split peas
7 cups chicken broth
$^1/_4$ cup butter
I chopped onion
3 minced garlic cloves
2 diced carrots
2 chopped celery stalks
2 bay leaves
I teaspoon basil
I large ham bone
2 teaspoons soy sauce
I teaspoon honey
I teaspoon salt
I teaspoon black pepper
$^1/_4$ cup chopped parsley

In a large pot, cover the split peas with the broth, and bring to a boil. Remove the peas from the heat, and let stand for about 75 minutes. In another large soup pot, sauté the onion and garlic in butter until all is tender. Add the carrots and celery, and sauté until they are tender. Stir in the peas and the remaining ingredients. Simmer the soup for 2 hours on low heat, stirring often. Check the soup for seasoning, and serve hot.

Blue Alaska Potato Soup

1 pound hamburger
4 cups potatoes, peeled and cut in $1/2$-inch cubes
1 chopped yellow onion
24 ounces tomato sauce
4 cups water
2 teaspoons garlic salt
1 teaspoon pepper
1 teaspoon hot sauce

In a large kettle, brown the hamburger and drain off fat. Add the potatoes, onion, and tomato sauce. Stir in the water, garlic salt, pepper, and hot sauce; bring the soup to a boil. Reduce the heat, and let the soup simmer for about 75 minutes, or until the potatoes are tender and the soup has thickened. Check the soup for seasoning, and serve hot.

Shady Meadows Camp Spicy Bean and Sausage Vittles

1 pound kidney beans
1 cup barley
1 pound sliced smoked sausage
7 cups chicken stock
2 chopped garlic cloves
3 bay leaves
1 teaspoon salt
1 teaspoon pepper

Rinse the beans, cover with cold water, and soak them for at least 12 hours. Drain off the water. Place the beans in a large kettle or pot. Cover the beans with water, and simmer on medium heat for about 45 minutes. Drain well. Place the beans, barley, sausage, stock, garlic, bay leaves, and pepper back into the pot, cover, and simmer on low heat for about 10 hours, stirring often. Remove the bay leaves, check for seasoning, and serve hot.

Swamp Shack Crayfish Chili

2 pounds hamburger
2 tablespoons bacon drippings
2 pounds crayfish tails
1 teaspoon chopped garlic
2 teaspoons salt
1 tablespoon soy sauce
1 teaspoon cayenne pepper
1 teaspoon dried mint
1 tablespoon parsley
3 tablespoons chili powder
8 ounces tomato sauce
1 cup dry white wine
1 cup beer

In a large saucepan, brown the meat in the bacon drippings. Combine the remaining ingredients, and bring to a low boil. Reduce the heat, and simmer while stirring often for about 4 hours.

Swamp Shack Crayfish Soup

1 chicken bouillon cube
1 cup boiling water
$1/4$ cup chopped onion
1 cup butter
3 tablespoons flour
$1/4$ teaspoon celery salt
$1/4$ teaspoon pepper
$1/4$ cup chopped parsley
1 quart milk
1 pound crayfish meat

Dissolve the bouillon cube in water. Cook the onion in butter until tender; blend in the flour and seasonings. Add the milk and bouillon gradually; cook until the soup is thick, stirring constantly. Add the crayfish meat; simmer on low for about 10 minutes. Check for seasoning, and garnish with parsley.

5

GRILLIN' AT THE CABIN

Without a doubt, the most popular cooking method at the cabin is grilling. And believe me, your old cousin Rick knows a thing or two about both! Nothing puts a smile on my tribe's faces faster than me cookin' up vittles on my Holland Grill. Here are some great grilling tips for you to use before we get started:

- Carbon monoxide and carbon dioxide are given off during combustion, so *never* barbecue indoors, as these odorless, toxic fumes may accumulate and cause health problems and death.
- Marinating quickly tenderizes meat and also adds flavor. Use roughly 2 cups of marinade for every 2 pounds of food. The marinade should completely surround the food. Cooked meat should *never* be returned to a cold marinade.
- My secret to tender, moist, tasty meat and fish is the cut I choose. The best cut for grilling steaks is a full one-inch thick.
- Trim beef steaks to $1/8$-inch fat. This reduces grease drippings to help minimize open flames. If you are like me and like your hamburgers juicy, go with ground beef that is about 15 percent fat. Have fish fillets cut from 1 to $1\frac{1}{2}$ inches thick. Anything thinner will dry out too quickly. Pork chops should also be at least 1 to $1\frac{1}{2}$ inches thick. This cut is cooked when the meat is no longer pink along the bone and when the juices run clear.

• For direct cooking on a charcoal grill, make sure there is enough charcoal to extend in a single layer 1 to 2 inches beyond the area of the food on the grill. Pour briquettes into the grill to determine the quantity, and then stack into a pyramid for lighting. For indirect cooking, place food over a drip pan and bank the briquettes either to one or both sides of the pan.

• When using charcoal, douse the coals with the least amount of starter fluid possible to light the fire. If starter fluid is unavailable, try using regular salad oil. Wad a sheet of newspaper and pile the coals over it, then douse the coals with the salad oil. Light the paper as you would using normal starter fluid.

• When roasting or grilling in a closed BBQ pit, open a can of beer and place the beer over the hottest part of the fire. The beer will boil and saturate the air inside the pit with water vapor, beer flavors, and alcohol. This will help in keeping the roasting meats moist, while adding flavor to the meat.

• Whenever barbecuing, use tongs to turn the meat. Never use a fork as it will punch holes in the meat and allow the natural juices to escape, causing the meat to lose flavor and become chewy.

• When grilling meats, it is usually best to turn the meat only once. When grilling meat to a medium or greater doneness, use the lid to assist in cooking. This will decrease the cooking time by applying heat to all sides of the meat at once.

• Tomato- or sugar-based BBQ sauces should be added only at the end of the grilling process, since they will burn easily and are seldom considered an internal meat flavoring.

Cozy Cabin Catfish Tidbits

2 pounds catfish fillets
I cup Worcestershire sauce
I cup soy sauce
I teaspoon cinnamon
2 tablespoons fresh ground black pepper
2 tablespoons garlic salt
I cup lemon juice
I sliced red onion

Cut the catfish fillets into strips. Mix together the Worcestershire sauce, soy sauce, cinnamon, black pepper, garlic salt, and lemon juice. Marinate the catfish strips in sauce for 6 hours in the cooler. Put the fillets on skewers with the red onion slices between fish slices, and cook on a charcoal grill for about 15 minutes, turning once.

Cousin Harvey's Grilled Salmon

$^1/_4$ cup soy sauce
$^1/_4$ cup rice wine vinegar
2 tablespoons sugar
I tablespoon vegetable oil
I teaspoon mustard powder
I teaspoon ginger
I teaspoon pepper
2 pounds salmon fillets

In a bowl, combine the soy sauce, vinegar, sugar, oil, mustard powder, ginger, and pepper. Place the salmon in a nonporous dish, and pour the marinade over the salmon. Cover, and marinate in the cooler for 2 hours, turning occasionally. Grill the salmon for about 4 minutes per side, or to desired taste. Check for seasoning, and serve hot from the grill.

Wood Tick Hound Dog Grilled Corn

$1/2$ cup softened butter
2 tablespoons chopped parsley
2 tablespoons chopped chives
$1/2$ teaspoon salt
$1/4$ teaspoon pepper
8 cleaned ears of corn

Blend the butter with the parsley, chives, salt, and pepper. Spread 1 tablespoon of butter mixture on each ear of corn. Wrap the corn individually in heavy foil. Grill the corn ears for about 20 minutes, turning every 5 minutes. Check for seasoning, and serve hot from the grill.

"Boys Been in the Whiskey" Grilled Shrimp

2 pounds unpeeled jumbo shrimp
I cup vegetable oil
I cup lemon juice
2 teaspoons dry Italian salad dressing mix
2 teaspoons seasoned salt
I teaspoon seasoned pepper
I teaspoon Worcestershire sauce
I tablespoon whiskey
4 tablespoons brown sugar
2 tablespoons soy sauce
$1/2$ cup chopped scallions

Mix the oil, lemon juice, salad dressing mix, salt, pepper, Worcestershire sauce, and whiskey. Place the shrimp in a large bowl, and cover with the marinade. Marinate in the cooler for 4 hours, stirring occasionally. Lift the shrimp from the marinade with a slotted spoon, and push onto skewers. Place the shrimp on a charcoal grill about 6 inches from the hot coals. Grill the shrimp for about 10 minutes, turning once and brushing with marinade. Pour the remaining marinade into a saucepan. Stir in the brown sugar, soy sauce, and chopped scallions. Heat to a boil. Dip the grilled shrimp into this sauce when serving.

Chopper's Hog Cabin Chops

³/₄ cup soy sauce
¹/₄ cup lemon juice
I tablespoon chili sauce
I tablespoon brown sugar
I minced garlic clove
6 pork loin chops

Combine the first five ingredients, place the chops in a dish, and pour the marinade over all. Cover and place in a cooler for 8 hours. Remove the chops from the marinade, and grill about 4 inches from the heat to desired doneness. Brush occasionally with marinade.

Cousin Rick's Cabin Ham

5 pounds boneless fresh ham pork leg
³/₄ cup chili sauce
¹/₄ cup red wine vinegar
2 tablespoons lemon juice
I teaspoon dry mustard
I minced garlic clove

Prepare the covered grill with drip pan in center, and bank with hot coals. Place the ham in the center of the grill. Grill over hot coals until the center of the ham registers 165 degrees with a meat thermometer, about 2 hours. Mix the remaining ingredients, and brush on cooking ham during the cooking process. Let the ham stand for 15 minutes before carving.

Grilled Cabin Balls

I pound hamburger

$^1/_4$ cup grated Parmesan cheese

2 cups chopped spinach, drained of any liquids

I minced garlic clove

I egg

I tablespoon garlic powder with parsley

$^1/_2$ teaspoon salt

$^1/_2$ teaspoon black pepper

$^2/_3$ cup cornmeal

Add the first eight ingredients together, and shape the meatballs to the size of an egg. Roll the meatballs in cornmeal, and grill on a greased rack for about 20 minutes, turning once. Check for seasoning, and serve the meatballs hot from the grill.

Doc Adam's Ribs

3 pounds short ribs

I tablespoon brown sugar

$^1/_4$ cup cider vinegar

2 cups chicken stock

2 cups water

$^1/_4$ cup ketchup

3 tablespoons tomato paste

I tablespoon dry mustard

I teaspoon Worcestershire sauce

$^1/_2$ teaspoon ground cloves

$^1/_2$ teaspoon chili powder

$^1/_2$ teaspoon cayenne

Place the sugar, vinegar, and ribs in a large pot, and cook for about 5 minutes. Add the stock, water, ketchup, tomato paste, mustard, Worcestershire sauce, cloves, chili powder, and cayenne. Cover and bring to a boil. Cook the ribs for about 25 minutes. Remove the ribs from the sauce, and place them in the cooler. Cook the sauce until it reaches desired thickness. Cook the ribs for about 20 minutes per side while basting with sauce.

Iowa Grilled London Broil

$1/2$ cup red wine vinegar
$1/2$ cup soy sauce
$1/2$ cup vegetable oil
$1/2$ teaspoon pepper
4 sliced garlic cloves
$3^1/2$ pounds London broil

Combine the vinegar, soy sauce, vegetable oil, pepper, and garlic in a dish, mixing well. Add the steak, turning to coat each side. Cover and marinate in the cooler for 8 hours. Remove the steak from the marinade. Grill the steak until desired tenderness, basting often with marinade.

Broken Porch Cabin Cutlets

$1/2$ cup vegetable oil
$1/4$ cup vinegar
$1/2$ teaspoon garlic salt
$1/2$ teaspoon pepper
1 tablespoon oregano
12 beef cutlets

Mix the oil, vinegar, garlic salt, pepper, and oregano. Flatten the cutlets. Pour the marinade over cutlets, and chill for 2 hours. Remove the cutlets from the marinade, and grill to desired tenderness while brushing with marinade.

Cobweb Cabin Steaks

4 boneless beef loin steaks
$^1/_3$ cup Dijon mustard
1 tablespoon chopped parsley
2 tablespoons honey
1 tablespoon cider vinegar
1 tablespoon whiskey
$^1/_2$ teaspoon Louisiana hot sauce
$^1/_8$ teaspoon black pepper
1 onion, cut into $^3/_4$-inch-thick slices

Combine the mustard, parsley, honey, vinegar, whiskey, hot sauce, and pepper. Place the steaks and onions on the grill grid over medium coals; brush both the steaks and the onions with the glaze. Grill the steaks and onions for about 12 minutes, turning once and brushing with glaze.

Cousin Rick's Cabin Burgers

1 pound hamburger
1 cup chopped mushrooms
$^1/_2$ cup chopped white onions
$^1/_4$ cup BBQ sauce (from *Grillin' Like a Villain* cookbook)
$^1/_2$ teaspoon Accent
$^1/_4$ teaspoon white pepper

Mix all the ingredients together, and make four large patties. Grill the patties to desired tenderness, and serve on large hamburger buns.

Canadian Cabin Steak

¹/₂ cup chopped yellow onion
¹/₂ cup lemon juice
¹/₄ cup olive oil
¹/₂ teaspoon Accent
¹/₂ teaspoon celery salt
¹/₂ teaspoon pepper
¹/₂ teaspoon thyme
¹/₂ teaspoon oregano
¹/₂ teaspoon rosemary
I minced garlic clove
3 pounds chuck steak, ³/₄ inch thick

In a large dish, combine all the ingredients together except the steak. Marinate the steak in the cooler for 4 hours, turning every hour. Remove the steak from the marinade, and grill over hot coals for about 30 minutes, turning once and basting with remaining marinade.

Mankato Springs Grilled Chicken

4 tablespoons olive oil
2 tablespoons rice vinegar
I tablespoon lemon juice
I tablespoon soy sauce
I tablespoon sugar
I tablespoon minced garlic
¹/₄ teaspoon ground ginger
¹/₂ teaspoon salt
¹/₂ teaspoon pepper
8 chicken thighs
I bunch green onions

In a mixing bowl, whisk together the oil, vinegar, lemon juice, soy sauce, sugar, garlic, ginger, salt, and pepper. Pour over the chicken meat, cover, and place in the cooler for 6 hours. Grill the chicken, skin side down, for about 20 minutes, turning once. Place the green onions on a skewer, brush with marinade, and grill for about 3 minutes per side. Serve the onions and chicken together.

Jeff and Linda's Deer Camp Grilled Chicken

3 cups frozen orange juice concentrate
1/2 cup Worcestershire sauce
1 tablespoon minced garlic
1 whole fryer chicken, cut up

Blend the orange juice, Worcestershire sauce, and garlic together, and pour over chicken pieces. Place the chicken in the cooler for 1 hour. Cook the chicken over low flames, basting with marinade, for about 30 minutes, turning once. The chicken is done when the juices run clear. Check the chicken for seasoning, and serve hot from the grill.

Rocky Top Chicken

2 teaspoons Dijon mustard
4 chicken breasts
1/2 teaspoon white pepper
1/3 cup butter
2 teaspoons lemon juice
1/2 teaspoon garlic powder with parsley
1 teaspoon tarragon

Spread the mustard on both sides of the chicken and sprinkle with pepper. Cover the chicken, and place it in the cooler for 2 hours. Melt the butter, stir in the lemon juice, garlic powder, and tarragon. Simmer on low heat for about 5 minutes, stirring often. Place the chicken on the grill, skin side down. Grill the chicken, basting with sauce, for about 60 minutes, turning and basting every 15 minutes.

My Holland Grill Chicken

8 chicken breasts
2 tablespoons olive oil
I tablespoon vinegar
2 tablespoons soy sauce
2 tablespoons honey
$1/2$ teaspoon thyme
$1/2$ teaspoon paprika
$1/2$ teaspoon cayenne
I tablespoon allspice
I teaspoon pepper
2 cups sliced mushrooms

Place the chicken in a dish. In a large bowl, combine the olive oil, vinegar, soy sauce, honey, thyme, paprika, cayenne, allspice, and pepper. Pour over the chicken, and place in a cooler for 2 hours. Remove the chicken, and grill for about 30 minutes per side. Pour the remaining marinade in a saucepan, add the mushroom slices, and simmer for 5 minutes. Spoon the sauce over grilled chicken breasts.

Mary Had a Little Cabin Lamb Chops

6 shoulder blade lamb chops
I cup minced mint
$1/2$ cup wine vinegar
2 teaspoons sugar
I tablespoon water
$3/4$ cup plain yogurt
I tablespoon Accent
2 minced garlic cloves

Mix all the ingredients together in a mixing bowl except the chops. Place 2 tablespoons of sauce into a small container, and add the water. Cover the container and place in the cooler. Cover the chops with the remaining marinade, and place the chops in the cooler for 6 hours. Grill the chops for 10 minutes, turning once. Drizzle the reserved marinade from the container over the cooked chops before serving.

First Night Quick Grilled Lamb

1 sliced garlic clove
1/4 cup olive oil
1/2 cup lime juice
1 tablespoon white pepper
6 lamb chops

Place the sliced garlic in the oil and allow to marinate for 6 hours. Combine the lime juice and pepper into the garlic oil. Marinate the chops in this dressing for 8 hours in the cooler. Grill the chops for 10 minutes, turning once. Check the chops for seasoning, and serve hot from the grill.

Wisconsin Dells Brats

6 bratwurst
1 cup beer
1/2 cup ketchup
1/4 cup water
1/4 cup minced onion

Combine the beer, ketchup, water, and onion in a saucepan, and simmer on low for 10 minutes. Grill the brats for about 10 minutes, turning once. Place the grilled brats in the sauce, and simmer for about 20 minutes on low. Serve the brats hot with the sauce.

Camp Vista Grilled Bratwurst

6 bratwurst

12 ounces beer

2 tablespoons brown sugar

2 tablespoons soy sauce

1 tablespoon prepared mustard

1 teaspoon chili powder

2 minced garlic cloves

$^1/_4$ teaspoon hot sauce

Mix all the ingredients together in a medium-sized saucepan, and simmer for about 20 minutes. Remove the bratwurst, and grill until browned. Return the grilled bratwurst to the marinade in saucepan, and simmer for 5 more minutes. Serve the cooked bratwurst on large French rolls with cooked sauerkraut.

Otter's Run Beef Brisket

1 cup white wine
3 cups apple cider
$^1/_2$ cup honey
2 tablespoons Dijon mustard
$^1/_4$ cup soy sauce
2 tablespoons brown sugar
2 tablespoons minced garlic
1 tablespoon minced ginger root
1 tablespoon coriander
2 sprigs thyme
2 pounds brisket of beef

Combine the wine, cider, honey, mustard, soy sauce, brown sugar, garlic, ginger root, coriander, and thyme in a heavy roasting pan. Add the beef brisket. Cover tightly, and place in a preheated 350-degree oven. Cook the brisket for about 60 minutes. Remove the brisket from the pan, cover, and set aside. Cook the juice in the pan over medium heat until it reduces to a glaze thick enough to coat the back of a spoon. Grill the brisket for about 60 minutes, turning twice and basting with the sauce from the pan. Let the beef stand for 15 minutes before carving. Serve the sliced beef with remaining sauce.

Crooked Arrow Burgers

2 eggs, beaten
2 tablespoons whipping cream
2 tablespoons milk
1 cup breadcrumbs
1 tablespoon minced onion
1 teaspoon Accent
2 teaspoons prepared horseradish
$1/4$ teaspoon pepper
$1/4$ teaspoon thyme
$1/2$ teaspoon dry mustard
2 pounds hamburger
$1/2$ cup butter
$1/2$ cup ketchup

In a large mixing bowl, stir in the eggs, cream, milk, bread-crumbs, onion, Accent, horseradish, pepper, thyme, and dry mustard. Mix together well, and let stand for 20 minutes. Add the hamburger, and mix in well. Melt the butter and ketchup in a saucepan, and keep warm. Make patties from the hamburger mixture, and grill until the patties reach desired tenderness while basting with reserved butter sauce. Serve the grilled burgers on large seeded buns.

Bubba's Shack-in-the-Woods Steak

3 cups consommé
²/₃ cup soy sauce
¹/₂ cup chopped green onions
8 tablespoons lime juice
4 tablespoons brown sugar
I minced garlic clove
2 cups dark beer
2 large flank steaks

In a large glass dish, combine the consommé, soy sauce, onions, lime juice, brown sugar, garlic, and beer. Add the steaks, and coat all sides with marinade. Let the steaks marinate in the cooler for 12 hours. Grill the steaks over hot coals for about 15 minutes, turning once. Check the steaks for seasoning, and serve hot from the coals.

Pleasant Hills Grilled Sirloins

6 beef sirloins
¹/₂ cup vegetable oil
¹/₄ cup lemon juice
¹/₄ cup red wine vinegar
¹/₄ cup black coffee
I teaspoon Dijon mustard
¹/₂ teaspoon curry powder
¹/₄ teaspoon rosemary
¹/₄ teaspoon thyme
¹/₄ teaspoon savory
I teaspoon salt
¹/₂ teaspoon white pepper

In a large dish, combine the oil, juice, vinegar, coffee, mustard, curry powder, rosemary, thyme, savory, salt, and pepper. Add the sirloins, and coat both sides of steaks. Let the steaks rest in the cooler for 4 hours, turning every hour. Grill the steaks on high for about 6 minutes per side. Check the steaks for tenderness, and serve.

Hungry Hunters' Chicken

3 pounds chicken breasts
1 cup bourbon
1 cup brown sugar
1 cup ketchup
6 tablespoons Worcestershire sauce
$^1/_2$ cup vinegar
3 tablespoons lemon juice
4 minced garlic cloves
1 tablespoon dry mustard
1 teaspoon seasoned salt
1 teaspoon pepper

In a bowl, combine the bourbon, sugar, ketchup, Worcestershire sauce, vinegar, lemon juice, garlic, mustard, seasoned salt, and pepper. Brush the chicken breasts with a thin coating of sauce, and grill the chicken for about 20 minutes, basting often with sauce. The chicken is done when the juices run clear.

Lot #13 Chicken

4 large chicken breasts
2 tablespoons cumin
2 tablespoons paprika
2 tablespoons brown sugar
1 tablespoon pepper
1 teaspoon curry powder
1 teaspoon cayenne
1 teaspoon salt
1/2 teaspoon seasoned salt
1 tablespoon Dijon mustard
1 tablespoon red wine vinegar
2 minced garlic cloves
2 teaspoons olive oil

Pat the chicken meat dry. Combine the cumin, paprika, brown sugar, pepper, curry powder, cayenne, salt, seasoned salt, mustard, vinegar, and minced garlic. Rub this mixture into the chicken several times to coat well. Brush the grill grate with olive oil. Place the chicken on the grill, skin side down. Cook for about 12 minutes per side, until chicken is just cooked through.

Swamp Witch Ribs

5 pounds baby backs
3 tablespoons paprika
1/2 teaspoon red pepper flakes
1 tablespoon garlic powder
2 teaspoons oregano
2 teaspoons thyme
1/2 teaspoon salt
1/2 teaspoon cumin
1/4 teaspoon nutmeg

Combine all the seasonings, and rub into all surfaces of the ribs. Grill the seasoned ribs for about 90 minutes, turning every 20 minutes.

Hungry Horse Cabin Chops

1/3 cup dry sherry
2 tablespoons soy sauce
1 tablespoon vegetable oil
1 teaspoon ginger root, minced
1 teaspoon honey
1 minced garlic clove
4 thick butterfly pork chops

In a large dish, mix together the sherry, soy sauce, oil, ginger root, honey, and garlic. Coat the chops on all sides, and place in marinade dish. Chill in the cooler for 2 hours. Grill the chops for about 20 minutes, turning once and basting with marinade. The chops are ready for serving when the meat is no longer pink in the center.

Campfire Chili Burgers

2 pounds ground beef or venison
1/2 pound Italian sausage
1/3 cup tomato-based chili sauce
Salt and pepper to taste

Set up your grill, and allow the coals to burn hot. When the coals are ready, lightly oil the grate. In a mixing bowl, mix together the ground meat, Italian sausage, chili sauce, salt, and pepper. Form eight balls, and flatten into square patties. Grill the patties for about 5 minutes per side, or until well done. Serve on buns with your favorite toppings.

Cabin Grilled Cheesy Treats

2 8-inch flour tortillas
2 tablespoons whole kernel canned corn, drained
5 ounces Colby–Monterey Jack cheese, shredded
1 thick-sliced tomato

Heat a skillet on the grill grate. Layer a tortilla with corn and cheese. Place the second tortilla on top. Heat on the grill until the cheese is melted and both tortillas are slightly brown. Top with the tomato slice, and serve hot.

Caribbean Cabin Kebabs

I got this recipe from the head beach chef while drinkin' rum from a coconut in Puna Cana, Dominican Republic. I loved the flavor so much, I now cook this recipe at least six times a year at the cabin.

12 large uncooked prawns, peeled and deveined
12 sea scallops, uncooked
12 fresh pearl onions, peeled
1 green bell pepper
1 cup mango curry sauce

Cut the bell pepper into twelve 1-inch squares. Cut the scallops into $1/2$-inch-thick pieces. Thread the prawns, scallops, onions, and green peppers onto four skewers, alternating the ingredients. Marinate the kebabs in mango curry sauce. Grill the kebabs for about 6 minutes, or until the scallops and shrimp are firm but still tender.

Garden of the Gods Ham Slice

1/2 cup extra-hot ketchup
1/2 cup orange marmalade
2 tablespoons finely chopped onion
2 tablespoons salad oil
1 tablespoon lemon juice
1 teaspoon dry mustard
1 very large ham steak

Combine all the ingredients except ham steak. Remove any fat from the edge of the steak, and broil over slow coals for about 15 minutes, turning once. Brush the steak with the sauce, and broil for another 15 minutes, turning and basting once. Heat the remaining sauce on the edge of the grill, and serve with the cooked ham steak.

Spanky Hoots Onions on De Grill

1 large yellow onion, peeled
2 tablespoons butter, melted
1 teaspoon minced garlic
Seasoned salt and pepper to taste

Mix together the minced garlic and butter. Set the peeled onion upright on a sheet of foil. Make several deep slices in the onion without cutting completely through it. Pour the garlic butter over the onion. Sprinkle with the seasoned salt and pepper to taste. Place the onion on the grill, and cook until the onion is soft, about twenty minutes. Serve hot from the grill with your favorite meat or as a meal on its own!

Jim Ferguson's Great American Outdoor Trails Cabin Brats

You can listen to Jim and your old Cousin Rick on the *Great American Trails Radio Magazine,* or visit www.gaot.net.

1 large foil bag
8 ounces fresh-cut fajita veggie mix
1 teaspoon Accent
1 teaspoon olive oil
6 beer bratwurst
Mayonnaise
Bratwurst buns

Set up the grill and coals for cooking. In foil grill bag, add the fajita veggie mix, Accent, oil, and beer brats; seal the bag. Toss gently to combine. When you are ready to grill, place the grill bag over the coals on cooking grate. Grill for about 12 minutes, turning once, until the brats are no longer pink and the veggies are tender. Serve brats on buns with mayo and grilled fajita veggies.

The Perfect Campfire Grilled In Old Nauvoo Cabin Burgers

2 pounds lean ground beef or elk
1 tablespoon Worcestershire sauce
2 teaspoons steak seasoning
2 ounces Nauvoo blue cheese, crumbled
2 ounces cream cheese, soft
4 large buns
Toppings to taste

Mix together the ground beef or elk, Worcestershire sauce, and seasonings, and divide into four meatballs. In another bowl, mash together the Nauvoo blue cheese and cream cheese to form a cheese paste. Divide into four cheese nuggets. Place a cheese nugget into the center of each meatball, and form into patties. Season with salt and pepper, and grill until desired doneness. Serve on grill-toasted buns with your favorite toppings.

Jeff Walker's Drunk Banana?

4 bananas
1 tablespoon lemon juice
1 cup brown sugar
1 teaspoon ground cinnamon
1 tablespoon Old Crow
2 cups vanilla ice cream

Halve each banana lengthwise, then widthwise. Sprinkle the bananas with lemon juice and Old Crow. In a bowl, mix together the brown sugar and cinnamon. Roll the banana pieces in the sugar and cinnamon mixture until well coated. Lightly oil the grill grate. Arrange the bananas on the grill, and cook for about 3 minutes per side. Serve in a bowl with vanilla ice cream topped with a sprinkling of the remaining cinnamon and sugar mixture.

Cabin Tidbits

Bacon
Sharp American cheese

Wrap 1-inch cubes of sharp American cheese in partially cooked slices of bacon. Rotate over coals until the bacon is done and the cheese is melted.

The Explorer Buffalo Tenderloin

4 tablespoons butter, soft
2 tablespoons chopped black olives
4 tablespoons diced roasted red pepper
4 large buffalo tenderloins
Seasoned salt and black pepper to taste
Olive oil

Combine butter, black olives, and peppers in a small bowl, and mash them together with a fork to combine well. Season to taste with seasoned salt and black pepper. Brush steaks with a little olive oil. Grill until desired taste. While the steaks are still hot, top each with a dollop of seasoned butter.

Mark and Rita Carlson's Garden Avenue Cabin Burgers

See, Snappy, I made you famous!

1 pound ground pheasant or quail
1/4 cup banana peppers, chopped and seeded
1/2 cup feta cheese, crumbled
Seasoned salt and white pepper to taste

In a medium glass bowl, mix the ground game bird, peppers, and feta cheese. Season with salt and white pepper. Form the mixture into four patties. Grill the patties about 10 minutes per side.

Take a large fan, and blow the flavored smoke towards Cousin Rick's house. Hurry up and eat before Cousin Rick shows up wantin' grilled game and cold beer!

Camp Basil Hazel Burgers

2 pounds lean ground sirloin
4 tablespoons Worcestershire sauce
2 tablespoons dried basil
$1/2$ teaspoon garlic salt
$1/2$ teaspoon white pepper
4 large seeded buns

In a medium bowl, mix the meat, Worcestershire sauce, basil, garlic salt, and white pepper. Form the mixture into four patties. Lightly oil the grill grate, and cook the meat for about 6 minutes, turning once, until desired doneness. Serve on seeded buns with your favorite camp toppings.

Colorado Marinated Venison Cubes

$1/2$ cup salad oil
$1/4$ cup vinegar
$1/4$ cup chopped onion
1 teaspoon salt
1 teaspoon coarsely cracked pepper
2 teaspoons Worcestershire sauce
2 pounds venison steak, cut in $1 1/2$-inch cubes

In a deep bowl, combine all the ingredients except venison steak; mix well. Add venison cuts to the marinade, and stir to coat. Refrigerate overnight, or let stand at cabin temperature 2 or 3 hours, turning meat occasionally. Grill until desired doneness.

Cousin Rick's Grillin' Like A Villain Camp Brats

4 fresh bratwurst sausages
$^1/_2$ cup Cousin Rick's BBQ sauce (from my *Grillin' Like a Villain* cookbook)

Fill a marinade injector with Cousin Rick's BBQ sauce. Inject the sauce into each bratwurst until the skin is tight. Place the bratwurst on the grill grate, and cook for about 10 minutes, turning once. Serve on grill-toasted buns with lots of fresh chopped onions.

Jimmy Buffet's Cabin Chicken

1 16-ounce package boneless, skinless chicken breast halves
$^1/_2$ cup Caribbean jerk marinade
1 cup mango peach salsa
2 tablespoons cilantro, chopped
1 small banana, diced

Combine the chicken and marinade in a small bowl; cover. Refrigerate for 2 hours, or until ready to grill. In a medium bowl, combine the salsa, cilantro, and diced banana. Place the chicken on the grill, and cook for about 20 minutes, turning once, until the chicken is no longer pink. Brush frequently with marinade during the first 10 minutes of grilling. Serve with the salsa.

Becky's Warm Cabin Buns

$^1/_4$ **cup butter, soft**
2 tablespoons prepared horseradish mustard
2 teaspoons poppy seeds
2 tablespoons finely chopped onion
4 hamburger buns, split
4 thin slices boiled ham
4 slices Swiss cheese

Mix the butter, mustard, poppy seeds, and onion; spread on cut surfaces of buns. Tuck a slice of ham and cheese in each bun. Place the sandwiches on foil, and heat on the grill until they are heated through.

Paula Sands KWQC Quad City Cabin Burgers

$^1/_2$ **cup shredded cheddar cheese**
1 tablespoon grated Parmesan cheese
1 chopped white onion
1 egg
1 tablespoon ketchup
1 tablespoon Worcestershire sauce
$^1/_2$ **teaspoon Accent**
Pepper to taste
1 pound lean ground beef
6 slices thick-cut smoked bacon
6 seeded buns, split

In a mixing bowl, mix together the cheeses, onion, egg, ketchup, Worcestershire sauce, Accent, and pepper to taste. Crumble in the ground beef, and mix together by hand. Form into six patties, and wrap a slice of bacon around each one. Secure the bacon with toothpicks. Place the patties on the grill, and cook for about 5 minutes per side, or until well done. Remove the toothpicks before serving on buns with your favorite toppings.

"That's All, Campers" Grilled Ham Steak

I large ham steak
¹/₄ cup apricot preserves
I teaspoon minced garlic
2 teaspoons Dijon mustard
Freshly ground pepper to taste

Cut the outer edge of the fat on ham diagonally at 1-inch intervals to prevent curling while cooking. Do not cut into the ham streak. Place the ham steak on the grill. Stir the remaining ingredients together in a small mixing bowl. Spread about half of the glaze over the steak. Grill for about 5 minutes, or until the glaze is bubbly and the edges are beginning to brown. Turn the steak, and spread with the remaining glaze. Grill for an additional 5 minutes, or until the glaze is bubbly and beginning to brown.

Lane County Cabin Grilled Quesadillas

8 flour tortillas
2 tablespoons olive oil
2 tablespoons Dijon mustard
2 green onions, chopped
2 red apples, cored and thinly sliced
2 cups shredded Gouda cheese

Brush oil onto one side of a tortilla, and place on a plate oil side down. Spread about ¹/₂ tablespoon of mustard on the top, and top with green onion, apple slices, and ¹/₂ cup of shredded cheese. Place a second tortilla on top, and brush the top with olive oil. Repeat with the remaining ingredients, stacking the quesadillas on the plate. Brush the grilling surface with oil, and place the quesadillas carefully in the grill. Grill for about 5 minutes, or until the bottom is crisp. Flip, and grill on the other side until good and crisp. Remove from the grill to serving plates, and cut into quarters. Serve hot to smiling, hungry campers.

Parkers Cabin Tacos

1 tablespoon fajita seasoning
1 teaspoon ground ancho chile
1 teaspoon ground cumin
1/2 teaspoon ground cinnamon
1/2 teaspoon red pepper flakes, crushed
1 very large sirloin steak
2 tablespoons extra virgin olive oil
Tortillas

In a small bowl, mix the fajita seasoning, ancho chile, cumin, cinnamon, and red pepper flakes. Rub the steak with olive oil. Sprinkle the spice mixture over the steak, and rub well. Grill the seasoned steak for about 15 minutes, turning once, or until desired taste. Remove the steak to a cutting board, and cover loosely with foil. Let the steak rest for at least 5 minutes. Slice it thinly in angled slices across the grain of the meat. Serve the steak covered with your favorite veggies and sauce wrapped in tortillas.

Camp Gobbler Burgers

1 pound ground turkey
1 tablespoon garlic powder with parsley
1 tablespoon red pepper flakes
1 teaspoon dried minced onion
1 egg
1/2 cup cheese-flavored crackers

In a bowl, mix together the ground turkey, garlic powder with parsley, red pepper flakes, minced onion, egg, and cheese crackers using your hands. Form into four patties. Place the patties on the grill, and cook for about 5 minutes per side, until well done.

Cabin Fever Squares

I loaf bread, unsliced
$^1/_4$ garlic clove, minced
$^1/_4$ cup butter, soft

Cut the loaf of bread into 2-inch cubes. Mix garlic and butter thoroughly. Spread the mixture on the outside of the cubes, and heat in foil over hot coals.

Snook's Montana Grilled Chicken

4 skinned chicken pieces
2 tablespoons oil
I tablespoon lemon juice
I tablespoon chopped thyme
2 cloves garlic, minced
Seasoned salt and pepper to taste

Fire up the grill, and allow the coals to turn red. Oil the grill grate. Meanwhile, mix the oil, lemon juice, thyme, and garlic. Place the chicken pieces in a shallow container, and cover with the mixture. Let it sit in the cooler or refrigerator for at least 30 minutes. When ready to grill, cook the chicken until tender and the juices run clear, turning every 10 minutes. Check the chicken for seasoning, and serve hot.

Cabin Lunch at Wilke's

1 can luncheon meat (Spam or Treet)
Canned sweet potatoes
Orange slices, quartered
$^1/_2$ cup brown sugar
$^1/_2$ cup orange juice
$^1/_4$ cup vinegar
1 tablespoon prepared mustard

Slice the meat into 1-inch squares, and string it onto skewers along with quartered orange slices and canned sweet potatoes. Cook over slow coals, turning frequently. Meanwhile mix together the brown sugar, orange juice, vinegar, and mustard. Brush the glaze on meat skewers, and cook for about 10 minutes, or until the glaze is brown and bubbly.

"That Was Easy" Lamburgers

2 pounds ground lamb
$^1/_2$ teaspoon salt
$^1/_3$ cup milk
5 strips smoked bacon

Combine the lamb, salt, and milk. Shape the mixture in five patties. Circle each with a strip of bacon and anchor ends with a wooden toothpick. Score the tops with a knife. Arrange the meat patties on grill. Cook for about 12 minutes. Turn the patties. Cook about 10 minutes longer, or until the patties are done.

Cousin Rick's Cabin Grillin' Like a Villain Bread

1 round loaf pumpernickel
$^1/_2$ cup soft butter
2 tablespoons prepared mustard
$^1/_2$ cup grated Parmesan cheese
$^1/_4$ cup snipped parsley

Cut the bread in $^1/_2$-inch slices. Mix the butter, mustard, cheese, and parsley; spread the mixture on the bread slices. Put the loaf together on a large piece of foil; cut the bread in half through the center, going almost to the bottom crust. Bring the edges of the foil over the loaf to cover. Heat at the side of the grill 20 to 30 minutes, or until hot, turning occasionally. Serve hot from the grill.

Hossteler's Cabin Dogs

2 tablespoons prepared mustard
16 ounces tomato sauce
$^1/_2$ cup dark corn syrup
$^1/_3$ cup vinegar
$^1/_3$ cup minced onion
2 tablespoons Worcestershire sauce
$^1/_2$ teaspoon celery seeds
$^1/_2$ teaspoon hot pepper sauce
1 pound frankfurters

In a skillet, blend mustard with a small amount of tomato sauce; add remaining tomato sauce along with the remaining ingredients, except franks. Cook over medium heat, stirring frequently, until the mixture comes to boiling; move it to the side of the grill, and simmer gently for about 30 minutes. Add the franks; cook until the franks are hot and plumped, 7 to 8 minutes. Serve the dogs hot with the sauce.

Nighthawk Grilled Sandwiches

12 slices pumpernickel
¹/₂ cup Thousand Island dressing
6 slices Swiss cheese
6 tablespoons drained sauerkraut
¹/₄ pound canned corned beef, sliced
Butter, soft

Spread six slices of bread with dressing. Top each with cheese, 1 tablespoon sauerkraut, corned beef, and bread slice. Butter top and bottom of sandwiches. Grill both sides until hot and the cheese is melted.

CABIN CAMPING SAFETY

Camping at your cabin should always be fun, relaxing, and full of excitement, but the right kind of excitement should not include accidents! No bites, burns, broken bones, or poison ivy.

The best way to have a safe and enjoyable camp is to be smart about safety.

Since you will have a copy of this book with you at your cabin, I thought it only fitting to include a few first aid pointers for quick reference at your fingertips.

Be prepared for the most common injuries with these easy first aid tips. Also, learn sensible strategies for preventing injuries in the first place. (Always have a well-stocked first aid kit available at your cabin.) I recommend you keep the following in your cabin first aid kit:

- ☐ Flashlight (with batteries)
- ☐ Whistle (for each cabin camper) to blow if you get lost and to keep large animals like bears and mountain lions away
- ☐ Tweezers for removing ticks and slivers
- ☐ Bandage tape
- ☐ Scissors
- ☐ Band-Aids
- ☐ Hydrocortisone cream

☐ Thermometer
☐ Burn ointment
☐ Matches or a lighter
☐ Antiseptic spray
☐ Ibuprofen
☐ A small first aid book

COMMON OUTDOOR HEALTH PROBLEMS

Strains and sprains: What's the difference between a strain and a sprain? Strains involve a partial tear of muscle. Sprains involve a partial tear of ligaments (which connect two bones) or tendons (which connect muscle to bone). **What Cousin Rick would do:** Stop activity immediately. Think of the acronym **RICE.** for the first forty-eight hours after the injury. (**R**)est: Rest the injured part until it's less painful. (**I**)ce: Wrap an ice pack or cold compress in a towel and place over the injury immediately. Continue for fifteen minutes at a time, six to eight times a day. (**C**)ompression: Support the injury with an elastic compression bandage for at least two days. (**E**)levation: Raise the injured part above heart level to decrease swelling. Take ibuprofen for pain and swelling. After forty-eight hours, apply a heating pad or moist heat three to four times a day.

Broken bones: You most likely have broken a bone if you heard a snap or a grinding noise during the injury; there is swelling, bruising, tenderness, or a feeling of pins and needles; it's painful to bear weight on the injured area or to move it. **What Cousin Rick would do:** Remove clothing from the injured part. Apply a cold compress or ice pack wrapped in cloth. Place a splint on the injured part. Seek medical care, and don't eat, in case surgery is needed.

Cuts: Most cuts can be safely treated at the cabin. Deeper cuts, or any wounds that won't stop bleeding, need emergency medical treatment. **What Cousin Rick would do:** Rinse the wound, and apply pressure to the cut with sterile gauze, a bandage, or a clean cloth. If blood soaks through, place another bandage over the first and continue applying pressure. Raise the injured body part to slow bleeding, but don't apply a tourniquet. When the bleeding stops, cover the wound with a new, clean bandage. To minimize scarring, apply sun block daily once the wound has fully healed.

Frostbite: Exposure to extreme cold can cause frostbite, which is a very serious condition that requires emergency care. Frostbite is more serious than frost nip. Frostbite often occurs on the hands and feet. Frostbite causes an aching pain or numbness. Frostbitten skin feels rock hard, with a white, waxy, or purplish appearance. **What Cousin Rick would do:** Get indoors immediately. Do not try to thaw frostbite unless you're in a warm place (warming and then reexposing frozen parts to cold can cause permanent damage). Remove wet clothing. Treat frozen parts gently; do not rub them. Warm the frozen body parts in warm (not hot) water for about 30 minutes. Do not use dry heat, such as a fireplace, oven, or heating pad, to thaw frostbite.

Heat exhaustion and heatstroke: During hot, humid weather, the body's internal temperature can rise, resulting in heat exhaustion. If not quickly treated, heat exhaustion can progress to heatstroke, which requires immediate emergency medical care and can be fatal. The signs and symptoms are severe thirst, muscle weakness, nausea, difficulty breathing, headache, increased sweating, clammy skin, weakness, dizziness, confusion, lack of sweating, and a body temperature of 105 degrees F or higher. **What Cousin Rick would do:** If the body temperature is 105 degrees F or more, or the person shows signs or symptoms of heatstroke, seek emergency medical care immediately. In cases of heat exhaustion, and while awaiting help, go indoors or into the shade immediately. Undress, lie down, and elevate the feet slightly. Take a cool bath, or get into a body of water. Take frequent sips of cool, clear fluids. Monitor body temperature.

Allergic reactions: Foods, medications, insect stings, pollen, or other substances can trigger allergic reactions. Although most allergic reactions aren't serious, severe reactions can be life-threatening and can require immediate medical attention. Signs and symptoms are itchiness, mild skin redness or swelling, stuffy or runny nose, sneezing, itchy and watery eyes, red bumps (hives) that occur anywhere on the body, swelling of the face or mouth, difficulty swallowing or speaking, difficulty breathing, abdominal pain and vomiting, and dizziness. **What Cousin Rick would do:** Contact a doctor if the allergic reaction is more than mild. Check with your doctor to see if you should carry an antihistamine such as diphenhydramine or epinephrine if you are allergic.

Tick bites: It's not uncommon to find a tick on your body if you're spending time in the timber. While most tick bites are harmless and don't require medical treatment, some ticks do carry harmful germs. The deer tick or western black-legged tick carries Lyme disease. These ticks are harder to detect than dog ticks because they're much smaller (an adult tick is about the size of a sesame seed). **What Cousin Rick would do:** If the tick is still attached to the skin, remove it with a pair of fine-tipped tweezers. Grasp the head of the tick close to the skin, and firmly pull the tick straight out of the skin. Do not twist the tick or rock it from side to side while removing it. Put the tick in alcohol to kill it. Wash your hands and the site of the bite with soap and water. Swab the bite with alcohol. Call the doctor if the tick has been on the skin for more than 24 hours, if part of the tick remains in the skin after attempted removal, if a rash develops, or if fever breaks out.

Spider bites: Most spider bites cause only mild reactions and can safely be treated at the cabin. Occasionally, though, a severe allergic reaction to spider bites can be life-threatening if left untreated. And some spider bites (such as those from the poisonous black widow and brown recluse spiders) need immediate care. Signs of a severe allergic reaction are swelling of the face or mouth, difficulty swallowing or speaking, tightening of the chest or difficulty breathing, dizziness or fainting, and abdominal pain or nausea. **What Cousin Rick would do:** If the person is bitten by a spider (other than a brown recluse or black widow) and doesn't seem to be having an allergic reaction, wash the bitten area with soap and water. Apply an ice pack or a cool wet cloth to the bite to relieve pain and swelling. Elevate the area to slow the spread of venom. Seek emergency medical care if he is showing any signs of an allergic reaction, such as developing any kind of rash after the bite, if the area begins to look infected (increasing redness, pain, swelling, warmth, or pus), or if you think the bite was from a brown recluse or black widow spider.

Animal bites: You love your cabin, and so do bats, raccoons, and skunks. The bad part about these little critters is that sometimes they can transmit rabies. Animal bites and scratches that break the skin can cause infection. Rarely, animal bites (particularly from wild animals) can cause rabies, a dangerous, life-threatening disease. **What**

Cousin Rick would do: Wash the area with soap and water, and apply pressure with sterile gauze or a clean cloth if the person is bleeding. (Do not apply an antiseptic or anything else to the wound.) Cover any broken skin with a bandage or sterile gauze. Seek emergency medical care if the person has a bite that punctured or broke the skin; the person was bitten by a wild or stray animal, or any animal that hasn't recently had rabies shots or is acting strangely; the person was bitten on the face, neck, or hand, or near a joint; the person has a bite or scratch that's becoming red, hot, swollen, or increasingly painful; the person is behind on immunizations (shots) or hasn't had a recent tetanus shot.

Sunburn: The best treatment for sunburn is prevention. Mild sunburn results in skin irritation and redness and can be safely treated at the cabin. Severe sunburn requires medical attention. **What Cousin Rick would do:** Remove the person from the sun right away. Place the person in a cool (not cold) shower or bath, or apply cool compresses several times a day. Avoid creams or lotions that may hold heat inside the skin or may contain numbing medication. Do not put butter or toothpaste on the burn. Offer the person extra fluids for the next two to three days. Give the person ibuprofen as directed, if needed, to relieve pain. Make sure all sunburned areas are fully covered to protect the person from the sun until healed. Call the doctor if the sunburn forms blisters or is extremely painful, the face swells from sunburn, the sunburn covers a large area, the person has a fever, severe chills, headache, confusion, or a feeling of faintness; the person has signs of dehydration (increased thirst or dry eyes and mouth); the person has signs of infection on the skin (increasing redness, warmth, pain, swelling, or pus).

6

WILD-GAME
COOKIN'

I have found that preparing wild game and fish at the cabin is never a dull topic. Everyone has their own special recipe that they have mastered throughout the years. Wild game does, however, have some cooking challenges, and you need to be creative when dealing with strong meat flavors. I always recommend that wild game should be prepared boneless with the fat trimmed and the silver skin removed.

A reader of one of my monthly outdoor columns once asked me if wild game is healthier than domestic meats. My reply? Heck yeah. Venison is a far cry better for you than beef. Less fat and cholesterol levels make venison the perfect diet meat. The only wild game I know of that is not as healthy for you as its domestic cousin is wild duck. Wild duck is higher in cholesterol than domestic chicken. However, if you're a lover of wild duck, like I am, you can get over that fact pretty quickly.

In this chapter I give you some of my favorite wild-game recipes I use at my cabin adventures. Enjoy!

Cliff's Canadian Bear Steak

1 cup flour
1 teaspoon salt
1 teaspoon pepper
1 teaspoon thyme
2 large bear steaks
1 cup sliced onions
5 tablespoons bacon drippings
2 cups beef stock
1 cup red wine
2 tablespoons tomato paste

In a bowl, combine the flour, salt, pepper, and thyme. Pound this mixture into all sides of the steaks using a meat hammer. Brown the onions in the bacon drippings, and add the seasoned steaks. Brown the steaks well on all sides. Add 1 cup of the stock and the cup of wine. Bring to a boil on medium heat. Reduce the heat, and simmer for 5 minutes. Turn the steaks, cover the pan, and let the steaks simmer on low for 2 hours, adding more stock if necessary. Check the steaks for seasoning, and serve.

Granny Black's Cabin Bear Roast

5-pound bear roast
2 teaspoons paprika
1 teaspoon Accent
$^1/_2$ teaspoon pepper
1 teaspoon seasoned salt
2 tablespoons minced onion
2 cups beef stock

In a small bowl, combine the paprika, Accent, pepper, and seasoned salt. Rub all sides of the roast with this mixture. Place the seasoned roast in a slow cooker, sprinkle with the onion, and pour the stock over all. Cook the roast on high for 2 hours, or until the roast is done and tender.

Turkey Camp Dumplings

6 cups chicken stock
1 26-ounce can cream of chicken soup
8 teaspoons butter
1 cup chopped onion
1 teaspoon salt
1 teaspoon pepper
8 flour tortillas
2 cups diced wild turkey, cooked

Bring the stock, soup, butter, onions, and seasonings to a boil in a large pot. Meanwhile, slice the tortillas into thin strips. Place the strips into the boiling broth, and cook for about 15 minutes. Add the turkey, and cook for another 15 minutes, uncovered.

Shaena Marie Ranch Cabin Goose

1 pair of goose breasts
$^1/_4$ cup flour
1 teaspoon salt
1 teaspoon pepper
$^1/_4$ cup bacon fat
$^1/_2$ cup milk

Skin the goose, and slice the whole breasts about $^1/_4$ inch thick, across the grain. Dredge in flour with the salt and pepper added to season. Fry the breast meat in hot bacon fat for about 1 minute on each side. Remove the meat from the pan, and stir in 3 tablespoons flour and milk to make gravy. Check the gravy for seasoning, and serve over fried goose meat.

Missouri Mel's Grouse

2 grouse breasts
I teaspoon celery salt
I teaspoon salt
I teaspoon pepper
$1/4$ cup bacon fat
6 chopped green onions
I cup chopped ham
I cup sour cream
$1/2$ cup chicken stock
3 tablespoons cooking sherry
I tablespoon parsley

Dust the grouse meat with celery salt, salt, and pepper. Cook the seasoned meat in bacon fat until golden brown on all sides. Add the onions, ham, sour cream, and chicken stock. Simmer for about 30 minutes. Add the sherry and parsley, check again for seasoning, and serve.

Green Bay Duck

3 duck breasts
2 cups milk
2 sliced onions
$1/4$ cup vegetable oil
I cup flour

Cut the meat from the breasts into $1/4$-inch-thick slices, and soak them in the milk for 8 hours. Drain the duck meat from the milk, roll the duck strips in flour, and fry in oil. Remove the fried duck strips, fry the onion slices, and serve over the fried duck meat.

Smitty's Mississippi River Cabin Duck Vittles

2 cleaned ducks
1 teaspoon salt
1 teaspoon pepper
1 chopped onion
2 chopped celery stalks
4 slices of bacon
3 cups water
1 teaspoon herb seasoning
2 chicken bouillon cubes

Preheat the oven to 300 degrees. Salt and pepper the duck meat. Place the seasoned meat in a baking pan. Add half of the onions and half of the celery; place the remaining celery and onions in body cavities. Strip bacon (two slices per bird) across the breasts. Add water, herb seasoning, and bouillon cubes to the pan. Cook at 300 degrees for about 3 hours, basting every 30 minutes. Check the meat for seasoning, and serve hot.

Alabama Slough Wild Duck

1 duck
1 sliced onion
$^{1}/_{2}$ cup butter
1 teaspoon salt
1 teaspoon pepper
2 cups water
1 bay leaf
1 cup sliced mushrooms
2 tablespoons flour
$^{1}/_{4}$ teaspoon thyme

Prepare and disjoint the duck. Place the duck in a large skillet, brown with onion, and baste with butter. Add salt, pepper, water, and bay leaf. Cook for 1 hour on low heat. Sauté the mushrooms, and add flour and thyme. Add to duck, and continue to cook for about 40 minutes.

Quail Cabin Supper

16 quail breasts
1 teaspoon bacon fat
1 diced yellow onion
2 cups cream of celery soup
¹/₄ cup sherry
¹/₄ teaspoon oregano
¹/₄ teaspoon rosemary
1 teaspoon salt
¹/₂ teaspoon pepper
1 cup sour cream

Place the cleaned quail breasts, meaty side down, in a large baking dish. Sauté the onions in the bacon fat in a saucepan, and add the soup, sherry, oregano, rosemary, salt, and pepper. Simmer for 20 minutes, and pour the mixture over the quails. Cover, and bake in a 350-degree oven for 60 minutes, turning every 10 minutes. Add the sour cream to the dove mixture, and stir to mix well. Bake uncovered for about 20 more minutes, and serve.

Becky's Hot Cabin Beaver

3 pounds cubed beaver meat
6 eggs, beaten
2 cups flour
1 teaspoon garlic salt
$^1/_2$ teaspoon white pepper
$^1/_2$ teaspoon ginger
$^1/_4$ teaspoon sage
$^1/_4$ teaspoon seasoning salt
1 tablespoon Accent
$^1/_4$ cup milk
$^1/_2$ cup vegetable oil

In a large mixing bowl, combine the eggs, flour, salt, pepper, ginger, sage, seasoning salt, Accent, and milk. Mix well until thin and smooth. Add the beaver meat, and coat well. In a large skillet, heat the oil until ready for cooking. Drop the individual seasoned meat cubes in the hot oil, and fry until all sides are brown. Check for seasoning immediately after cooking, and serve.

Becky's Hot Cabin Snapper

2 pounds cubed turtle meat
$^1/_2$ cup vinegar
1 teaspoon salt
$^1/_2$ cup flour
$^1/_4$ cup milk
2 eggs, separated
2 teaspoons olive oil
$^1/_2$ teaspoon seasoned salt
$^1/_4$ cup vegetable oil

In a large saucepan, combine the turtle meat, vinegar, and salt. Cover with water, and simmer for about 70 minutes. Drain, and allow to cool. In a large mixing bowl, combine the flour, milk, egg yolks, olive oil, and seasoned salt; mix well. Beat the egg whites until stiff, and fold into batter. Dip the turtle cubes into batter, and fry in vegetable oil until brown on all sides. Check the meat for seasoning, and serve.

Niota Frogs in the Cabin

5 pounds frog legs
$^3/_4$ cup vinegar
1 cup milk
6 eggs
2 tablespoons vegetable oil
$^1/_4$ teaspoon seasoned salt
2 cups flour
1 cup vegetable oil

Place the frog legs in a large container with the vinegar. Cover the container, and chill 4 hours. In a mixing bowl, combine the milk, eggs, 1 tablespoon vegetable oil, and seasoned salt. Mix into a smooth batter. Season the chilled frog legs with salt and pepper, dip each leg into the batter, and then coat each with flour. Fry the legs in hot vegetable oil until brown on all sides. Check for seasoning, and serve.

Cactus Katie's BBQ Rattlesnake

1 large rattlesnake, freshly skinned, head removed
1 cup BBQ sauce (from *Grillin' Like a Villain* cookbook)
1 teaspoon Accent
1 teaspoon cayenne

Cut the snake into bite-sized chunks. Marinate the snake pieces in BBQ sauce for about 2 hours. Wrap the seasoned snake in heavy foil, and grill for about 50 minutes, basting every 15 minutes or so. Check the meat for seasoning, and serve.

Shimmy Trees Squirrel

2 dressed and cleaned squirrels, cut into serving-sized pieces
1 teaspoon seasoned salt
$^1/_2$ teaspoon pepper
$^1/_2$ cup flour
$^1/_2$ cup vegetable oil
$^3/_4$ cup chicken stock
2 cups milk
1 tablespoon minced onion

In a bowl, combine the seasoned salt, pepper, and flour. Dredge the meat, and coat all sides. Heat the oil in a heavy skillet; brown the meat slowly on all sides. Add the chicken stock, cover skillet, reduce heat, and simmer on low for about 30 minutes. Remove the meat, cover, and keep warm. Blend remaining flour into the skillet drippings. Add the milk and onions, and simmer while stirring to make a great-tasting gravy. Serve the meat with hot gravy.

Bubba's Baked Tree Rats

4 squirrels, cut into serving-sized pieces
4 cups canned mixed vegetables
4 cups cream of mushroom soup
2 cups buttermilk
$^1/_2$ cup melted butter
2 cups flour

In a large pot or kettle, boil the squirrel meat for about 60 minutes. Remove the meat from the bones when drained and cooled. In a large baking dish, combine the vegetables, soup, and meat. In a bowl, combine the buttermilk, butter, and flour; pour this mixture over the meat mixture. Season with salt and pepper, and bake in a 350-degree oven for about 60 minutes.

The Stumble Inn's Donnellson Rabbit

2 rabbits, cut into serving-sized pieces
2 cups flour
$^1/_2$ tablespoon seasoned salt
$^1/_2$ teaspoon white pepper
10 tablespoons bacon drippings
$^1/_2$ cup water
2 teaspoons vinegar
1 chopped yellow onion

Combine the flour, seasoned salt, and pepper in a plastic bag. Add the rabbit meat, and shake to coat the meat pieces on all sides. In a large skillet, brown the rabbit meat in the bacon fat. Add the water, vinegar, and onions. Cover the skillet, and simmer for 30 minutes on low.

Stone Grove Pheasant

2 pounds pheasant breast, boned and cubed
1 cup pancake flour
$^1/_4$ cup butter
1 cup diced onion
2 cups diced celery
1 cup diced carrots
3 cups chicken broth

Dust the pheasant meat with pancake flour, and brown in butter in a large skillet. Add the onions, celery, carrots, and broth. Simmer for about 60 minutes on low heat. Season with salt and pepper, and serve with gravy from skillet.

Christmas Country Pheasant

2 pheasants, cleaned and dressed
$^1/_2$ teaspoon salt
$^1/_2$ teaspoon pepper
2 tablespoons olive oil
I cup white wine
I cup half-and-half
$^1/_2$ cup butter
I ounce brandy
I chopped yellow onion
$^1/_4$ cup sliced mushrooms
3 bay leaves
$^1/_4$ teaspoon thyme
$^1/_4$ teaspoon caraway
2 cups sour cream
I teaspoon Worcestershire sauce
3 tablespoons lemon juice

Season the bird meat with salt and pepper, and place in a large pot. Brown the meat on all sides in olive oil. Remove the meat from the pot. Stir in the wine and half-and-half. Stir well, and simmer for 20 minutes on low heat. Remove the pot from the heat, and add the remaining ingredients. Simmer for another 20 minutes. Add the cooked pheasant meat, and simmer on low heat for another 60 minutes.

Pointers Bites

1 pheasant, cut into chunks
1 cup flour
2 tablespoons cornstarch
2 tablespoons Parmesan cheese
2 tablespoons parsley
1 teaspoon Accent
1 cup beer
2 eggs
1 teaspoon seasoned salt

In a mixing bowl, combine the flour, cornstarch, cheese, parsley, Accent, beer, eggs, and salt. Mix the batter well. Dip the meat chunks in batter to coat well. Deep fry until the juices run clear. Check for seasoning, and serve.

Arkansas Cabin Possum

1 possum, skinned and cleaned
1 teaspoon garlic salt
1 teaspoon pepper
2 tablespoons bacon fat
1 chopped white onion
1 cup seasoned breadcrumbs
1 teaspoon Worcestershire sauce
1/4 cup white wine
4 slices salt pork

Dust the possum with garlic salt and pepper. Brown the onion in bacon fat. Add the seasoned breadcrumbs, Worcestershire sauce, and wine. Simmer for about 5 minutes on low heat. Stuff the possum with the mixture, and place in a deep baking dish, belly side down. Place the salt pork slices over the top of the meat, add about 1 quart of water to dish, and roast for about 3 hours in a 325-degree oven, basting every 20 minutes.

Mountain Man Fried Muskrat

1 large muskrat, skinned and cleaned
$^1/_4$ cup cider vinegar
1 teaspoon seasoned salt
$^1/_2$ teaspoon white pepper
1 sliced yellow onion
$^1/_2$ cup bacon fat
1 cup ketchup
1 teaspoon Worcestershire sauce
2 cups chicken broth

Soak the muskrat for 12 hours in 2 quarts of water and cider vinegar. After soaking, cut into serving-sized pieces. Place the meat in a large pan, and add 1 quart of water, salt, pepper, and onion. Cook the meat for about 60 minutes. In a large skillet, brown the cooked muskrat in bacon fat on all sides. Pour the ketchup and Worcestershire sauce over browned meat, add 2 cups chicken broth, and simmer for about 40 minutes to make a great-tasting gravy.

Lake Wyoconda Crow

3 crows
1 tablespoon lard
1 pint beef stock
1 teaspoon garlic salt
1 teaspoon pepper
$^1/_2$ teaspoon cayenne
$^1/_2$ cup sliced mushrooms
2 tablespoons cream

Clean and cut the crows into small portions, and cook them a short time in the lard in a large saucepan—be careful not to brown them. Add the beef stock, garlic salt, pepper, and cayenne. Simmer on low heat for about 60 minutes. Add the mushrooms and cream. Simmer for another 15 minutes on low heat and serve.

Cousin Crandall's Wild-Game Woodchuck Recipe

1 large woodchuck
1 cup flour
3 tablespoons bacon fat
1 tablespoon salt
1 teaspoon pepper

Clean the woodchuck, and cut into serving pieces. Boil the meat in a large pot with salted water for 60 minutes. Remove the meat from the water, and coat with flour. Fry the meat in bacon fat until golden brown on all sides, and season with salt and pepper.

Freeman's Illinois Cabin Cooked Polecat

3 skunks, skinned and cleaned
Beer to cover meat
3 egg yolks, beaten
2 cups milk
2 cups flour
2 tablespoons salt
2 tablespoons garlic powder
2 tablespoons baking powder
2 cups vegetable oil

Cut the skunks into small serving-sized pieces. Place the meat in a large pot, cover with beer, bring to a boil. Cook the meat for about 45 minutes. Remove all the scum that rises to the surface. Make batter by mixing together the egg, milk, flour, salt, garlic powder, and baking powder. Heat the oil in a large fryer, dip the pieces of skunk in batter, and fry them until golden brown.

Montana Venison

2 pounds venison roast
2 chopped onions
2 teaspoons turmeric
4 teaspoons ginger
2 teaspoons salt
I chopped garlic clove
$^1/_2$ cup vegetable oil
I cup canned tomatoes, drained
2 cups onion soup

In a large dish, combine the onions, turmeric, ginger, salt, garlic, and roast. Let stand in the cooler for 4 hours. Sauté the roast in oil in a large pan. Drain the fat, and add the tomatoes and soup. Cover and simmer on low heat for about 2 hours, adding water if needed.

Deer Balls

2 pounds deer burger
$^1/_2$ cup seasoned breadcrumbs
I minced onion
$^1/_3$ cup milk
I egg
I minced garlic clove
I teaspoon salt
I teaspoon pepper

Mix all the ingredients together, and shape into $^1/_2$-inch meatballs. Cook in hot oil until the meatballs are brown on all sides and the centers are no longer pink.

Country Cabin Fried Deer Steak

1 large venison steak
1 teaspoon garlic salt
$1/4$ cup flour
1 tablespoon bacon fat
$1/2$ cup water

Season the steak with salt and roll in flour. Brown the steak in bacon fat in a large skillet. Add the water, cover, and simmer until the meat is tender. Use the drippings for great-tasting gravy.

Broke Hunter's Deer Vittles

1 pound deer burger
1 diced onion
1 diced green pepper
1 teaspoon black pepper
1 teaspoon garlic salt
4 cups pork and beans

Brown the deer burger, onion, and green pepper. Stir in the pepper, garlic salt, and beans. Simmer on low for about 15 minutes, and serve.

Cousin Rick's Cabin Loins

6 deer loins
$^1/_4$ cup flour
1 teaspoon salt
1 teaspoon pepper
2 tablespoons butter
$^1/_2$ cup sour cream
1 tablespoon Worcestershire sauce
1 teaspoon celery salt
1 bay leaf

Season the flour with salt and pepper. Roll the loins in seasoned flour. Melt the butter in a large skillet, and brown the loins on both sides over medium heat. Pour the sour cream over browned loins, and add the Worcestershire sauce, celery salt, and bay leaf. Cover the skillet, and simmer for about 20 minutes.

Sir Williams's Venison Burgundy

2 pounds cubed venison steak
$^1/_4$ cup butter
1 chopped onion
2 chopped carrots
$^1/_4$ teaspoon thyme
2 tablespoons flour
1 chopped celery stalk
1 cup burgundy wine
1 cup water

Brown the venison in butter. Add the remaining ingredients, and simmer on low heat until the sauce thickens and the veggies are tender. Check the meat and sauce for seasoning, and serve.

BUBBA'S BAD CABIN CAMPING TIPS
(Remember, Bubba's not the coldest beer in the cooler.)

• When using a public cabin campground, a tuba placed on your picnic table will keep the cabins on either side vacant.

• Get even with a bear that raided your cooler by kicking his favorite stump apart and eating all the ants.

• Old socks can be made into high-fiber jerky by smoking them over an open fire.

• When smoking fish, never inhale.

• A hot rock placed in your sleeping bag will keep your feet warm. A hot enchilada works almost as well, but the cheese sticks between your toes.

• The best backpacks are named for national parks or mountain ranges. Steer clear of those named for landfills.

• Acupuncture was invented by a camper who found a porcupine in his sleeping bag.

• While the Swiss Army knife has been popular for years, the Swiss Navy knife has remained largely unheard of. Its single blade functions as a tiny canoe paddle.

• Effective January 1, 2007, you will actually have to enlist in the Swiss Army to get a Swiss Army knife.

• Lint from your navel makes a handy fire starter. Warning: Remove lint from navel before applying the match.

• You'll never be lost if you remember that moss always grows on the north side of your compass.

• You can duplicate the warmth of a down-filled bedroll by climbing into a plastic garbage bag with several geese.

• When at the cabin, always wear a long-sleeved shirt. It gives you something to wipe your nose on.

• You can compress the diameter of your rolled-up sleeping bag by running over it with your truck.

• Take Bubba's simple test to see if you qualify for solo camping. Shine a flashlight into one ear. If the beam shines out the other ear, do not go to the cabin alone.

• A potato baked in the coals for one hour makes an excellent side dish. A potato baked in the coals for three hours makes an excellent hockey puck.

- In emergency situations, you can survive in the wilderness by shooting small game with a slingshot made from the elastic waistband of your underwear.
- The guitar of the noisy teenager at the cabin next door makes excellent kindling.
- Check the washing instructions before purchasing any apparel to be worn at the cabin. Buy only those that read, "Beat on a rock in stream."
- The sight of a bald eagle has thrilled outdoorsmen for generations. The sight of a bald man, however, does absolutely nothing for the eagle.
- Bear bells provide an element of safety for hikers in grizzly country. The tricky part is getting them on the bears.
- In an emergency, a drawstring from a parka hood can be used to strangle a snoring cabin mate.

7

CABIN CAMPING SNACKIN'

I wrote this chapter mainly for the cabin rugrats to enjoy. Some of my best childhood memories of my parents' cabin involved helping dad and mom make great-tasting snacks. However, don't think for one buck-in-rut minute that the cubbies of the cabin enjoy cooking and eating camping snacks more than the big bears. Take time to teach the little campers the fun of cooking, and they too will remember the time spent with you at the cabin. Who knows, they just might grow up and write a best-selling cabin cookbook too!

Stink Bait

1 cup butter
1 cup Parmesan cheese
5 cups toasted oat cereal
1 teaspoon Accent
$1/2$ teaspoon garlic powder with parsley

Heat the butter in a large skillet until melted; remove from heat. Stir in the cheese; add the cereal. Sprinkle with seasoning, and mix thoroughly.

Bear Curds

18 ounces peanut butter
1 cup melted butter
2 cups confectionary sugar
3 cups crisp rice cereal
6 ounces melted chocolate chips

Mix all the ingredients together, except the chocolate chips. Roll the dough into meatball-sized balls, and let them stand in the cooler for 2 hours. Dip each ball into the melted chocolate chips, and allow the coating to harden.

Hiker Bars

1 tablespoon butter
25 large marshmallows, diced
2 tablespoons peanut butter
4 cups high-protein cereal

In a large saucepan, melt the butter. Add the diced marshmallows; heat and stir until the mixture is good and melted. Remove the pan from the heat; stir in the peanut butter. Add the cereal, and mix well to coat. Press the mixture out on a large cookie sheet, and allow to cool. Cut the shapes and sizes of your bars.

Hobo Fudge

1 pound powdered sugar
3 ounces cream cheese
8 tablespoons soft butter
$^1/_2$ cup cocoa
1 teaspoon vanilla

Place all the ingredients together in a large plastic bag, and using your hands, mix the ingredients together for about 8 minutes. Shape the fudge into squares, and serve.

Chipmunk Droppings

1 cup dry-roasted peanuts
1 cup diced dried fruit mix
1 cup chocolate chips

Combine all the ingredients together, and toss well.

Goldie Locks Mix

2 cups whole-grain wheat and raisin squares
4 cups animal crackers
2 cups mixed dry fruit pieces
1 cup candy-coated milk chocolate pieces

In a large bowl, combine all the ingredients together for a great hiking snack.

Werewolves Tummy Fillers

2 cups unsweetened puffed corn cereal
2 cups toasted oat cereal
1 cup fish-shaped cheese crackers
1 cup chow mein noodles
3 tablespoons vegetable oil
1 tablespoon dry buttermilk salad dressing mix

In a large bowl, combine all the ingredients together, except the vegetable oil. Toss well, and place the mixture on a baking pan. Sprinkle the mixture with vegetable oil. Bake in a 350-degree oven for about 12 minutes, turning twice. Season to your liking, or eat as is.

Daddy's Favorite Cabin Pineapple

1 whole pineapple
8 tablespoons butter
1 teaspoon cinnamon

Cut the pineapple in half, then into wedges, discarding the rind. Melt the butter, and add the cinnamon in a small saucepan. Grill the pineapple wedges on medium heat, basting with butter and cinnamon mixture, until the fruit turns golden brown and has softened.

Cabin Kids' Rice Pudding

1 cup instant rice
$1/2$ cup dry milk
$1/4$ cup raisins
2 tablespoons sugar
$1/4$ teaspoon cinnamon
$1 1/2$ cups water

Put the ingredients into a zip-top bag and mix. Bring $1 1/2$ cups water to a boil. Add the contents of the bag, and stir thoroughly. Remove from heat, cover, and let sit, stirring occasionally, for about 8 minutes.

Can You Dig It Scones

2 cups flour
1 teaspoon baking powder
$^1/_2$ teaspoon salt
6 tablespoons frozen butter
$^1/_2$ cup sour cream
1 egg
$^1/_2$ cup fruit

In a large mixing bowl, combine the flour, baking powder, and salt; cut in the butter with pastry blender, and add the sour cream and egg. Stir in the fruit. Place the mixture on a floured surface, shape into two 8-inch circles, $^1/_2$ inch thick. Cut each circle into eight wedges and place on an ungreased cookie sheet. Bake for about 15 minutes in a 400-degree oven until lightly browned.

Come Back Yeller Popcorn

6 cups popped popcorn
2 tablespoons sugar
2 teaspoons water
$^1/_4$ teaspoon cinnamon
$^1/_8$ teaspoon ground ginger
$^1/_8$ teaspoon nutmeg

Spray an unheated baking pan with cooking spray. Place popped popcorn in the baking pan. Stir together the sugar, water, cinnamon, nutmeg, and ginger in a mixing bowl. Add the spice mixture to the popcorn. Toss the popcorn to coat well. Bake in a 350-degree oven for about 15 minutes, stirring twice. Allow the popcorn to cool before eating.

Grandma Black's Camping S'mores

2 slices graham crackers
3 tablespoons oleo
25 large marshmallows
2 chocolate candy bars

Grease a cookie pan. Break the graham crackers into bite-sized pieces and place in bottom of pan. In a saucepan, melt the oleo and marshmallows until the mixture becomes like a syrup. Pour the mixture over the broken crackers. Flatten out on bottom of pan. Break the chocolate bars into bite-sized pieces and stick into mixture. Place the pan in the cooler for about 20 minutes. Cut the bars, and eat them up.

Coyote Chow

3/4 cup peanut butter
1 cup chocolate chips
1/4 cup butter
8 cups wheat flakes cereal
2 cups powdered sugar

Place the powdered sugar in a large brown paper sack, and set aside. Melt the peanut butter, chocolate chips, and butter together in a saucepan over low heat. Place the cereal in a large bowl, and pour the chocolate mixture over the cereal, stirring evenly to coat. Pour the chocolate-coated cereal into the powdered sugar sack, and shake well to cover.

Nighttime Nachos

I pound ground beef
$^1/_4$ cup chopped yellow onion
I cup pork and beans
$^1/_2$ cup homemade BBQ sauce
I bag nacho cheese flavor corn chips
$^1/_2$ cup grated cheddar cheese

Brown the ground beef and onions in a pan and drain fat. Add the beans and BBQ sauce. Heat thoroughly. Place a serving of chips on a plate and top with beef mixture and then grated cheese.

Campfire Candy

I cup chocolate chips
$^2/_3$ cup sweetened condensed milk
I tablespoon water
$^1/_2$ cup granola cereal

In a saucepan, combine the chocolate chips, milk, and water. Melt over low heat, stirring constantly. Remove the mixture from heat when the chips are melted, and pour into a foil-lined square pan. Sprinkle the top with granola cereal. Let stand for 2 hours, and then cut into small squares and serve.

Campfire Grilled Treats

4 slices of bread
2 tablespoons chunky peanut butter
2 bananas
2 chocolate candy bars
8 large marshmallows, diced

On a piece of bread, spread 1 tablespoon of peanut butter. Place 5 slices of banana, 3 small chocolate squares, and 3 diced marshmallows on top. Cover with another piece of bread, and place in a greased pie iron. Do the same again with the remaining ingredients. Cook over a campfire until the bread is golden brown, and the center is good and melted.

BBQ Worms and Beetles

2 tablespoons butter
2 teaspoons BBQ seasoning
I cup mixed nuts
¹/₂ cup chow mein noodles

In a large saucepan, combine the butter and BBQ seasoning. Place on medium heat, and melt butter. Stir in the mixed nuts and chow mein noodles. Cook, uncovered, on medium heat for about 5 minutes, stirring every 2 minutes until the mixture is good and toasted. Spread the cooked mixture on a large sheet of foil, and allow to cool for 30 minutes before eating.

Campfire Ghost Story Treats

2 cups applesauce
$1/2$ teaspoon cinnamon
$1/3$ cup raisins
$1/3$ cup chopped walnuts
$1/2$ cup red cinnamon candies
I cup whipped dessert topping

In a small saucepan, combine the applesauce, cinnamon, raisins, and nuts. Cook over medium heat until hot, stirring occasionally. Spoon into dessert dishes. Sprinkle with red cinnamon candies, garnish with whipped topping, serve while scaring your campfire friends.

Ye Olde Ants on a Log

5 stalks celery
$1/2$ cup peanut butter
$1/4$ cup raisins

Cut the celery stalks in half. Spread peanut butter over one side of the stalks. Sprinkle with raisins, and let the kids tear them up!

Johnny Reb's Cabin Peanuts

5 pounds raw peanuts, in shells
I 6-ounce package dry crab boil
I 4-ounce can sliced jalapeño peppers, with liquid

Place the peanuts in a slow cooker. Sprinkle with dry crab boil. Cover with water. Stir in sliced jalapeño peppers and liquid. Cover the slow cooker, and cook the peanuts on low for about 10 hours, or until the peanuts float to the top of the water.

Cabin Rockin' in the Timber Taco Dip

I pound hamburger
³/₄ cup water
I I ¹/₄-ounce package taco seasoning mix
I 16-ounce can crushed tomatoes
I pound loaf processed cheese, shredded

In a large skillet, brown the hamburger, and drain the fat. Stir in the seasoning packet and water. Bring to a boil; reduce the heat to a simmer. Let cook for about 5 minutes, stirring occasionally. Place the meat mixture into a slow cooker. Add the tomatoes and cheese, and cook on low for about 60 minutes. Serve with tortilla chips.

Cabin Cocktail Smokie Sauce

I cup grape jelly
I cup Dijon mustard
¹/₄ cup ketchup
³/₄ cup brown sugar
4 16-ounce packages little smokies

In a slow cooker, mix the jelly, mustard, ketchup, and brown sugar. Place the little smokies into mixture, and simmer for about 2 hours.

Critter Dip

2 pounds hamburger
I chopped onion
I 10³/₄-ounce can cream of mushroom soup
I pound processed cheese, cubed
I 12-ounce jar sliced jalapeño peppers, drained

Place the hamburger and onion in a large skillet over medium heat. Cook until the meat is browned and the onions are tender. Drain the fat, and turn the heat to low setting. Pour in the soup. Mix in the cheese cubes and jalapeños. Cook and stir for about 20 minutes. Serve with corn chips.

'Shrooms

2 cups soy sauce
2 cups water
I cup butter
2 cups sugar
4 8-ounce packages fresh button mushrooms, stems removed

In a saucepan over low heat, mix together the soy sauce, water, and butter. Stir until the butter is melted, and add the sugar. Stir together until the sugar has dissolved. Place the mushrooms in a slow cooker, and add the sauce. Cook on low for about 8 hours, stirring every hour. Place the cooked mushrooms in the cooler, and chill before serving.

Tortilla Bean Dip

2 I I ¹/₂-ounce cans of bean and bacon soup
I I-ounce package taco seasoning mix
8 ounces sour cream
¹/₄ cup salsa
¹/₂ cup shredded cheddar cheese

Place the soup, seasoning mix, sour cream, and salsa in a slow cooker, and mix well. Top with cheese, and cook on low for about 1 hour, or until the cheese has melted. Serve with tortilla chips after a long day of outdoor cabin fun.

Fall Apple Dip

I 8-ounce package cream cheese
¹/₂ cup brown sugar
I tablespoon vanilla extract
Apple slices

In a large mixing bowl, combine the cream cheese, brown sugar, and vanilla. Mix well until all of the brown sugar has been blended. Dip the apple slices into mix, and enjoy.

Corny Cabin Dogs

2 8¹/₂-ounce packages cornbread mix
2 tablespoons brown sugar
2 eggs
1¹/₂ cups milk
1 cup grated cheddar cheese
8 hot dogs, cut in half

Preheat the oven to 400 degrees. Lightly grease muffin tins. In a mixing bowl, stir together the cornbread mix and brown sugar. In a small bowl, whisk together the eggs and milk, and then stir into the dry mixture until moistened. Mix in the cheese. Spoon mixture into muffin tins until they are two-thirds full. Add half a hot dog to each muffin. Bake for about 16 minutes, or until golden brown.

Marvin's Little Camping Smokies

1 pound sliced bacon, cut into thirds
1 12-ounce package little smokies
³/₄ cup brown sugar

Preheat the oven to 325 degrees. Refrigerate the bacon. It is easier to wrap the smokies with cold bacon. Wrap each smokie with a piece of bacon, and secure with a wooden toothpick. Place on a large baking sheet. Sprinkle brown sugar over all. Bake for about 40 minutes, check for seasoning, and serve.

Camp safely,
—Cousin Rick Black

INDEX

ABOUT THE AUTHOR

Rick Black is a veteran hunter, fisherman, and outdoor cook. He has written several bestsellers from wild-game cooking to barbequing and how-to books on hunting and fishing.

He has a weekly spot on the *Great American Trails Radio Magazine* and writes the "Cousin Rick Says" column for the *Fort Madison Daily Democrat* and *Keokuk Daily Gate City* newspapers.

Rick is very active in many state and regional outdoor associations—he is a committee member for Des Moines County, Iowa, Pheasants Forever, Chapter 271; vice chairman for Friends of the N.R.A. (Des Moines County, Iowa, chapter); and senior chairman for Iowa Hunters for the Hungry. Rick is also an author for several monthly outdoor columns in Iowa newspapers.

Rick has served as president/sergeant of a police department reserve unit. He and his wife of over 22 years, Becky, are longtime residents of southeast Iowa.